UP*close:*

ROBERT F.★ KENNEDY

a twentieth-century life by
MARC ARONSON

VIKING

VIKING

Published by Penguin Group

Penguin Young Readers Group, 345 Hudson Street, New York, New York 10014, U.S.A.

Penguin Group (Canada), 90 Eglinton Avenue East, Suite 700, Toronto, Ontario,
Canada M4P 2Y3 (a division of Pearson Penguin Canada Inc.)

Penguin Books Ltd, 80 Strand, London WC2R 0RL, England

Penguin Ireland, 25 St Stephen's Green, Dublin 2, Ireland (a division of Penguin Books Ltd)

Penguin Group (Australia), 250 Camberwell Road, Camberwell, Victoria 3124, Australia
(a division of Pearson Australia Group Pty Ltd)

Penguin Books India Pvt Ltd, 11 Community Centre, Panchsheel Park, New Delhi – 110 017, India

Penguin Group (NZ), 67 Apollo Drive, Mairangi Bay, Auckland 1311, New Zealand
(a division of Pearson New Zealand Ltd.)

Penguin Books (South Africa) (Pty) Ltd, 24 Sturdee Avenue, Rosebank, Johannesburg 2196,
South Africa

Penguin Books Ltd, Registered Offices: 80 Strand, London WC2R 0RL, England

First published in 2007 by Viking, a division of Penguin Young Readers Group

10 9 8 7 6 5 4 3 2 1

LIBRARY OF CONGRESS CATALOGING-IN-PUBLICATION DATA

Aronson, Marc.

Up close : Robert F. Kennedy / by Marc Aronson.

p. cm.

ISBN 978-0-670-06066-5 (hardcover)

1. Kennedy, Robert F., 1925–1968—Juvenile literature. 2. Legislators—United States—Biography—
Juvenile literature. 3. United States. Congress. Senate—Biography—Juvenile literature. 4. Kennedy
family—Juvenile literature. I. Title.

E840.8.K4A76 2007   973.922092—dc22   [B]   2006102150

Set in Goudy Old Style   Book design by Jim Hoover   Printed in U.S.A.

973.922092
Aro
Y

Contents

Foreword

JOHN KENNEDY WAS assassinated the week I was to have my Bar Mitzvah. To everyone I knew he had been the symbol of hope, and his murder cast a shadow on the adult life I was just beginning to imagine. When Robert Kennedy ran for the Senate in New York, my parents did not like him. They saw him as an opportunist, nothing like his brother. I agreed. But years later I began to hear of another Bobby. For the generation of people younger than I am, John Kennedy was a figure from history, a person from long ago. Bobby was their hero. My wife tells me her immigrant father wept when he heard Bobby had been shot.

So who was Bobby? Pale shadow of his brother? Ambitious conniver? Crusader for the poor and unfortunate? Martyr?

I wrote this book to try to make sense of a person people either hated or loved. And then something else happened. The more I wrote about him, the more

I found myself writing about the 1960s. I came to feel that the contradictions in Bobby were also the different faces of that tumultuous age, a time when we were full of energy and anger, hope and delicious rage. I loved having the chance to explain what those years were like to young readers who know them only from retro fashions, old songs, or textbooks.

Finally, my twenty-first-century life shaped this book as much as my teenage years. When I learned that the world was nearly destroyed in 1962 because the only way the Soviets in Washington could reach Moscow was by handing a telegram to a bicycle messenger, I realized that Bobby's biography was also the story of the beginning of the digital age. His life spanned from the age of movie and radio to the dawning of the Internet. It was exciting to see his story anew, not just as a reflection of the Cold War and the politics of protest but as a step in the growth of media and communications.

I hope all of these impulses—making sense of the bad Bobby and the good, passing on a sense of the sixties, linking Bobby's story to the digital age—come through to you, my readers. Most of all, this was fun to write. I hope that comes through, too.

Introduction

Monday, June 3, 1968

BOBBY KENNEDY IS on the campaign trail, the one white politician who plunges into poor neighborhoods where armed Black Panthers speak openly of rebellion. He wants that challenge. He is the marshal, the gunslinger, who will bring order into the country—even if he has to bend the rules and cover his tracks to do so. Yet he also seems so real, so unguarded he is almost a saint. The two qualities—ruthlessness and vulnerability—are joined in one word: he is fearless.

Kennedy is wiry and short. In black-and-white pictures there often seems to be a shadow across him—like a tough street fighter from an old movie who can instantly flip into rage: Jimmy Cagney, Humphrey Bogart, early Jack Nicholson. Sean Penn has some of that aspect today: a sense of edge. You don't want to mess with this guy; he can "go off" in an instant. But in color photos, there is a different man. Though not blond, he has the tousled Kennedy hair. You can picture him playing touch football; you can *imagine him out on the waves; you see him tumbled in a heap with his pregnant wife and ten children. There is something softer, but also charmed, about him. He has the strange trait of alternately seeming hard as nails and shy. That is the magic of Bobby Kennedy.*

Bobby has one last day to appeal to the whole state of California, to keep his chances of being nominated for president alive. If he wins the Democratic primary tomorrow, all things are possible. Bobby has one last day to run as hard as he can, past the doubters, the critics, his own exhaustion, toward victory. Picture a movie that captures that last day of campaigning. It would have to move as fast as he did; he spent the day, as he spent his life, running.

Bobby, in Los Angeles with his family, took six kids to Disneyland the day before. Today he flies up to San Francisco's Chinatown. It's the morning of a workday; the streets are packed four deep. Kids rush out onto the streets to trot alongside his car. Bobby and his wife Ethel are in an open car, a convertible; he must have it that way, so that he can feel the crowd, and they can almost touch him. Suddenly five, six shots ring out. Ethel slumps down. Bobby doesn't flinch. Keeps waving. Just a string of loud firecrackers. Bobby makes sure Ethel is okay, drives on. Now to Fisherman's Wharf, to give a lunch talk at DiMaggio's, a restaurant owned by the great baseball player.

He flies back down the coast to Los Angeles; he is to mingle with people in a park. But six thousand have gathered to hear him, so he makes up a speech. Bobby is drained, doesn't feel well, but pushes himself on. Drives up through Watts, the black section of Los Angeles where he is a hero, then on to Venice, a beachfront community lined with canals and odd houses straight out of cartoons. Everywhere there are crowds, filling the streets on the way to the airport. People must see Bobby, be near him, feel him.

Bobby is hope. Bobby is peace—an end to the horrible Vietnam War. Bobby is the one politician the despairing can listen to, can believe in. He is electric, and everyone who is hurting needs to get close, to feel the current.

Last stop, San Diego. So many supporters they can't fit into the hotel. Bobby speaks, but is exhausted, has to sit down, buries his head in his hands. Comes out, gathers himself, and ends by quoting George Bernard Shaw:

"Some men see things as they are and say, 'Why?' I dream things that never were and say, 'Why not?'"

He is done. Finally, by eleven P.M., he, his wife, and

six of their children travel to a friend's home by the beach. He can rest.

One day. Twelve hundred miles. Speeches made to every color of Californian. Mexicans, blacks, the poor, the outcast, have cheered Bobby with all their hearts. He has given everything, every ounce of himself.

The next day, a man who did not join in the cheering will head out to the range, to practice shooting his revolver.

Chapter
★ 1 ★

HIS BROTHER JACK leans back, straight as a board, counterbalancing the wind. *Flash II*, Jack calls his trim Star Class boat, whose sails billow like the stylish dresses of well-brought-up debutantes. Cutting through the waves of Nantucket Sound, Jack does seem like a flash of light, darting at a faster pace than anyone around him. Bobbing in their slower boats, the old Protestant families mutter to themselves. The sons and daughters of Joseph Kennedy love to sail, fast. Too fast, say those guardians of old wealth, proud of their bloodlines stretching back to colonial days. They cheat, those Catholic Kennedys and their conniving father, say the Protestant families. Jack doesn't mind. Nor does Joe Jr., Jack's older brother, who is just a bit better at everything than everyone else. The third brother—ten years younger than Joe, and eight than Jack—Bobby, with the name that sounds so girlish, so sweet, Bobby cannot swim.

Tom Mix, wearing the white hat, was one of the most popular stars in Hollywood. In 1926, the year after Bobby was born, Joseph Kennedy (on the left) became the head of a movie studio. Joseph was a powerful man and his children were thrilled that he knew movie stars. But he was also often far away from his family.

Self-made, an extremely wealthy man, Joseph Kennedy has decided: Joe Jr., the wonder boy, will be the first Catholic president of the United States. Jack is being groomed, too, to glide comfortably into the world of the most important men and most beautiful women. Joseph hardly notices Bobby, born after Joe Jr., Jack, Rosemary, Kathleen, Eunice, and Patricia, and before Jean and Ted. Except, that is, to call him a "runt."

The runt of the litter is the one who may not make it, who might not even survive. Bobby is the little one who can hardly stand on his own feet, who keeps crashing into things. His hands tremble. He even looks scared, as if he had just been knocked down, bruised, and doesn't want to cry.

Bobby hates every moment of being seated with his sisters at the girls' end of the table. He hates fumbling with everything he touches. He hates the word "sissy" that even the older women whisper about him. He even hates being called "Bobby." He hates all of it, and he won't stand it another second.

As the story goes, he is about four years old, out on the boat in Nantucket Sound. He might be small and clumsy, but he has his father's clear, cold blue eyes—the gaze of absolute determination. Perhaps he squeezes those steely eyes for just a second, then:

Bobby dives.

He will learn to swim, damn it, or drown.

It doesn't matter which.

Over and over, Bobby leaps off the boat.

Each time, the ever-perfect Joe Jr. rescues him.

"It either showed a lot of guts or no sense at all," the more cool and distant Jack, now President John Kennedy, later joked.

A lot of guts or no sense at all, that was Bobby Kennedy. The runt on his wobbly legs is cute. But Bobby didn't want to be cute. He would catch up, and then win, or be destroyed. "Nothing came easy to him," a friend later said of Bobby. "What he had was a set of handicaps and a fantastic determination to overcome them." Bobby himself put it best: "We were to try harder than anyone else," he said of all the Kennedy children. "We might not be the best, and none of us were, but we were to make the effort to be the best."

"We were to"—the family was like an army unit, a clan that had absolute orders from on high. No individuals, no excuses, no mercy. Joseph Kennedy, the commander in chief, made that mission absolutely clear: "We don't want any losers around here. In this family we want winners. . . . Don't come in second or third—that doesn't count—but win."

Every second was a contest, which Bobby entered with reckless fury. Being dismissed by his father, eclipsed by his brothers, that was torture. What did it matter if he hurt himself diving off a boat? He was hurting already.

Joseph Kennedy was not a screamer. He didn't have to yell at his children to make his point. He used his eyes. When he stared straight at you, peering over his glasses, your blood ran cold. "Daddy's look," it was

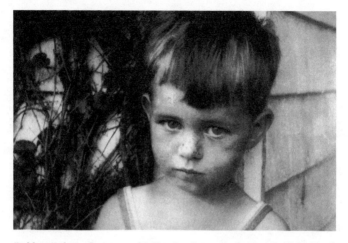

Bobby at about five years old. People often talked about Bobby as both shy and tough, easily hurt yet a battler who would never give in. That is exactly how he looks here.

called, and it silenced a raucous household. Daddy set the rules. And one rule was that you were to be prompt, to arrive at family dinners precisely on time.

Bobby is five now, playing in the living room of the family's large home in Bronxville, a nice suburb near New York City. Joseph has made millions on Wall Street, and this is the right place for a successful stock trader to live. His home is well appointed, with a grand staircase leading up from the ground floor.

Dinner. Dinner is announced.

Bobby is playing in the living room.

Dinner.

Bobby jumps up.

Bobby runs headfirst into the thick plate glass under the stairway that separates the living room from the dining room.

His face streaked with blood, glass fragments flying everywhere. Bobby is swept off to the doctor for stitches.

Bobby would do anything not to disappoint his father. Diving into cold water, smashing into plate glass meant nothing to him—compared to failing the man with icy blue eyes like his own. Years later, when he was twenty-two, he took James Noonan, a friend, out sailing on a twenty-five-foot Wianno Senior. Specially designed to fare well in the waters around Cape Cod, these boats can be handled by up to four sailors. This time there were just two, or really one: James was along for the pleasant trip, but hardly knew a sail from a sheet. Maybe Bobby was eager to be with a friend, having a good time, just the two of them together. But, suddenly, he realized that it was getting far too close to lunch hour to depend on the winds to bring him back on time. So he turned the boat in the right direction and dove off.

Bobby swam away, with stroke after confident stroke taking him back to the family. He would arrive, dripping wet, in time not to disturb his father. But he had abandoned James out on the water. When James finally managed to bring the boat in, Bobby's only reaction was, "terrific, but we've got to do something about your sailing."

A boy who drives himself mercilessly expects no less from others. No soft voice soothed Bobby's aches, so he had none to offer another. That, too, was Bobby Kennedy: the relentless, reckless third son of a clan determined to change history.

Reckless courage was a characteristic Robert Francis Kennedy showed throughout his life. The bigger the challenge, the more eager he was to throw himself at it. As a child, Bobby flung himself into cold waters. As a lawyer in Washington, and later as attorney general, he took on the nation's most dangerous mobsters. He went up, one-on-one, against Jimmy Hoffa, a corrupt union official who was as ruthless as he was powerful. At the height of white racial violence, Kennedy made himself the number-one target of armed and hate-crazed segregationists. Then at the worst moment of African American fury and despair he chose to speak in an all-black neighborhood. In a time when assassinations of outspoken leaders were all too common, he plunged into endless crowds. Bobby Kennedy was fearless. And yet he would never, ever, defy his family. He would do anything to be a great Kennedy, but would never question the obligations of being a part of that tragic clan.

Bobby was blessed and cursed by being born a Kennedy. His father was a strong, shrewd, confident man who impressed the most important leaders in America. Everyone from the president in Washington to the richest businessmen on Wall Street to the heads of Hollywood studios eagerly answered his phone calls. But Joseph did not work so hard only for himself. He was ready to devote every penny he earned to providing for his family and opening the world to his sons. No one, not even a royal prince, was born into the world with as much family support behind him as the sons of Joseph Kennedy. That was the blessing Bobby received from his father. But it came with a price.

Bobby was and would always be a Kennedy. He could—in fact, he must—use all of his ability, his skill, his courage, to make a difference in the world. He was free to challenge his father's ideas. But everything he did from the day he was born to the day he died would be with the family, and for the family. He was an individual, but really he was part of a group, and everything he ever did must serve that group. Bobby was trapped inside the family that made him special. That was the family curse.

This book, then, is the story of Bobby but, equally, of the Kennedy family. And there is something especially appropriate about that. America is often called the land of opportunity. Ever since the first Europeans crossed the Atlantic, America has been described as a place where a single person, on his own, could make his fortune. That is only partially true. The old established families lived in an America defined by ancestry, not individual effort. And Americans who were not white, or Protestant, or from old families had more limited horizons of opportunity. Bobby Kennedy's fate was to be the product of a wealthy family, but a family whose religion made them outsiders. He enjoyed the best of the land of opportunity, but was a spokesman for the victims of prejudice. As he struggled with these contradictions, he tried to craft a new future for the country. In that sense his story was not just that of a man and a family, but of a nation coming of age.

fine. Jack needed twenty-eight stitches to put himself back together.

Today, many families would treat a bloody crack-up like this as an alarm bell, a sign of trouble in Joe Jr., in Jack, in the home. All of that would prove true. Joe's competition with his brother *was* out of control. Jack *was* battered, brutalized, and could never show it. Instead he treated the injuries the same way he would later deal with his serious illnesses: staying cool, bemused, distant, and keeping them hidden from sight. In fact, Joseph *was* putting the family under tremendous strain. But for the Kennedys, as for most people in the 1920s, injuries like Jack's were just the normal mishaps of boyhood.

In their relentless determination, Joe and Jack were following perfectly in their forefathers' footsteps. Patrick Kennedy was one of the desperate Irish who fled from the potato famine that ravished their homeland in the 1840s. He accomplished his main goal: he reached Boston and managed to survive. But when he died in 1858, he left his wife, his son Patrick Joseph, and three daughters with nothing. At fourteen, young P.J. had to quit school to start making money. A hard worker and a good businessman, he figured out how to profit by catering to the needs of his fellow Boston Irish. He bought one, then a second, then a third tavern, followed by a liquor-importing business. As he rose in the community, he made a name for himself as a good listener who was ready to help out if someone needed a little cash. P.J. converted this popularity into a political career, first running for office himself, then becoming an important behind-the-scenes power broker.

P.J.'s life was a remarkable success story, a tribute to his hard work and good sense. But for those who disliked the Irish, it merely reinforced their prejudices. Rose Fitzgerald, who went on to marry P.J.'s son Joseph, described this split very well. Boston's leading old Protestant families "lived serenely amid ancestral portraits and mahogany sideboards and silver tea services in spacious houses on large grounds. With the advantages of inherited wealth and status and close-knit interfamily ties, they controlled the banks, insurance companies, the big law firms . . . and almost all the usual routes to success."

These families had a sense that they were the true Americans, and certainly the rightful masters of their city and state. They saw the poor, uneducated, Catholic

Irish as recent arrivals who drank too much and were too clannish. When hiring workers, these proud Protestants made clear that "no Irish need apply." Whatever his accomplishments, P.J. was an Irish innkeeper, and not welcome in the inner circles of Boston.

Joseph, P.J.'s son, was the trailblazer who brought the Kennedys into the world of the old Boston families. He went to Harvard, not just because it was a good school but because that was the place for the sons of Boston's elite. Joseph knew that everyone was judging him, seeing him as a Catholic outsider, the child of a family of barkeeps. Indeed there have been endless stories that Joseph actually made his money as a bootlegger, smuggling in liquor from Canada during Prohibition, but there is no proof. On Wall Street he definitely did manipulate stock prices in ways that would now be illegal. But at the time, he was just cooler, smarter, tougher than the old-money men, and he beat them at their own game. He expected nothing less of his sons.

If Joseph conquered the Protestant world of wealth and privilege, what was left for his children? His daughters were groomed to marry well. What of his sons? Only one Catholic had ever been a serious candidate for president. And when Al Smith ran in 1928, millions of Americans had made it clear that they were not ready to accept a Catholic in that high office. That did not faze Joseph, who had already selected Joe, his firstborn, his namesake, to run the whole country. The Kennedy family had not been defeated by the potato famine or by Boston snobbery. If the Kennedy men were relentless, they were fighting not just for themselves but to change history.

There were actually two families within the Kennedy household. Joseph's wife Rose put her own strong stamp on the nine children, especially Bobby and the younger girls. Rose was the daughter of John F. Fitzgerald, which made her a leading light of what might be termed Boston Catholic royalty. "Honey Fitz" was one of the nation's most capable politicians. Blessed with a fine voice, and brilliant at charming voters, Honey Fitz was elected mayor of Boston. That made him the first person of Irish heritage to reach that position in any American city. Like Joseph, Rose had been reared by a family determined to prove that an Irish Catholic could be as well brought up as the most established Protestant. But a woman's role was thought to be very different from a man's. While Joseph had been groomed for Harvard, Rose was forbidden to attend

Wellesley. Instead she was sent to convent schools to study with nuns.

Rose was intelligent, strong, and hardworking. In these ways she was the perfect partner for Joseph. But they were also quite different. For one thing, her religion was as important to her as success in the world was to him. Bobby, the younger son, the sensitive one whose face only looked tough until you noticed that the sneer was halfway to tears, was his mother's "favorite," her "little pet."

Joseph the invincible patriarch and Rose the queen of organization reigned together each night at the family dinner table. Every meal was a lesson for children being groomed to rule. Rose prepared the novices, filling bulletin boards with clippings from newspapers and magazines. As she explained, "The girls and boys . . . were supposed to read or at least scan these in order to be able to say something about the topics of the day" at dinner. Then came the tests. When the children were younger, Rose ran the quizzes. She would read from a newspaper piece on the state of Florida to "ask how the state got its name. What does the word mean, and what language is it from?" As Joe and Jack got older, Joseph took over.

The Kennedy family dinner table became an on-going seminar on politics and policies, where all were expected to know their facts and current events, and Joseph constantly challenged his older sons. When Joe or Jack asked a question about world affairs, he would respond in detail, as if speaking to adults. Then he would take challenging positions just to see how quick they were on their feet. Perhaps Bobby, quiet, seated with the younger girls, was racing through names and dates to think of a way to join in, but no one would have considered pausing to give him a chance. Meal-time conversations were as much a test of guts and will as were daytime bicycle races.

While Joseph had strong, generally conservative opinions, he knew his sons could only become leaders if they were exposed to men with different points of view. One after another, they were packed off to visit all corners of the world, even the Communist Soviet Union. Joseph realized that his sons had to see the world and think for themselves.

Yet for all of Joseph's commitment to opening the minds of his children, he also passed along his preju-dices. He did not like Jews, and did not hide it. Even though Catholics also experienced discrimination, he did not want Harvard to remove the quota system that severely limited the number of Jews it admitted. His children listened. When Joe Jr. visited Hitler's Germany in 1934, he was impressed with the Germans' pride and "great spirit." He knew that Jews were being forced out of their jobs, but believed the Germans when they said this was a necessary response to the Jews' "unscrupulousness."

Joseph's intellectual curiosity and his private biases were not just a family matter, for in 1938 President Franklin D. Roosevelt appointed him ambassador to England. This was a crowning achievement. Now the grandson of a man who had fled starvation in Ireland would be calling on the king of England as America's representative. And this just as Hitler dared the entire world to bow to him or defeat him.

In March, Rose herded five of her children onto the *Manhattan* to sail across the Atlantic and join her husband. Joe was at Harvard, where he would graduate in the summer, with Jack to follow two years later. Bobby would not turn thirteen until November, but, on this trip, he was the eldest boy. That might have been a

At eleven, Bobby is both the properly dressed prep-school boy and the kid who can't wait to put on his roller skates.

wonderful opportunity. But looking back on the trip, it really revealed the impossible pressures in Bobby's life.

Bobby kept plotting and planning to find a way to bring a Bronxville pal with him to England. "I'll write you," they each swore, sounding like characters in a novel about summer camp. Even as the *Manhattan* was getting ready to pull away from the dock, Bobby tossed one last message out the porthole to his friend. But he steamed away with his mother, leaving his friend behind.

In London, Bobby acted the gentleman. He stopped traffic so that the family nanny could easily cross busy streets. The nanny was needed because Rose had so many official duties. That made Bobby all the more attentive to her. Whenever they traveled, he was careful to sit next to her. A boy just on the edge of adolescence, he would rush to the door each night when his mother went out, in order to tell her she looked beautiful. He was the perfect young man, the escort, at the service of his mother.

Once a day, he and his younger brother Teddy (who had turned six in February), were each granted an hour alone with their father. This daily audience was

Bobby's only moment for quiet conversation with the great man. Finally, this was Bobby's chance to have the kind of discussion that he had heard each night at the dinner table. But Joseph did not seem to expect much from Bobby, which only drove his son to strive ever harder to win his attention. Even years later Bobby pleaded with his father to continue to speak to him, on paper: "I wish Dad that you would write me a letter as you used to Joe and Jack about what you think about the different political events and the war as I'd like to understand better than I do now."

Joseph had a great deal to say about politics, for Adolf Hitler was making clear that he was ready to go to war to capture a part of Czechoslovakia in which there were many Germans. As the leading American spokesman in Europe, Joseph was a crucial voice. England was debating whether to take a stand against the dictator. What was America's position? Was it also willing to challenge Hitler? Not Joseph Kennedy. He was horrified by the thought of a second world war, and passionately in favor of what came to be called "appeasement"—giving in to Hitler. Americans, he argued in October of 1938, should get along with dictators, not antagonize them.

Joseph arrives in England to take up his appointment as American ambassador. He is flanked by his two elder sons, Joe Jr., on the left, and John, on the right. Bobby was forever trying to catch up to and impress this trio of glamorous men.

Less than a month after Ambassador Kennedy spoke, on the night of November 9, Nazis went on an organized rampage against Jews in Germany. On Kristallnacht—the Night of Broken Glass—Jewish homes and shops, thousands of them throughout the country, were plundered. Jews were raped, murdered, thrown into jail. Germans were like beasts turned loose on their prey. This was the true face of Hitler's Germany. Alarmed, Kennedy suggested organizing a global program to get Jews out of Germany. But the plan went nowhere. And everyone now knew him as the man who would rather bend to Hitler than resist him. Being the ambassador to England was no longer an honor for Kennedy; instead it exposed him to increasing condemnation.

Bobby was not in London to see his father under attack. He had returned to America with his mother and younger siblings, and was then sent off to boarding school. Not only was he under tremendous internal pressure, he was alone.

★ ★ ★

The school stands on a hill overlooking Rhode Island's Narragansett Bay, open to the winds. Today, beautiful buildings and a well-groomed campus make Portsmouth Abbey a welcoming place to be a student. But when Bobby was sent to what was then Portsmouth Priory, conditions were much more primitive. Thin walls did little to keep out the chill, and shivering students tacked up blankets as makeshift storm windows. They were on their own, toughing out the cold, just as they needed to fend for themselves against other students. When Teddy followed Bobby there two years later, he told his brother that he was being picked on. "You'll just have to look out for yourself," Bobby warned. He knew, because he had been through the fire.

Black-robed monks guided students at the priory— which you can picture as a kind of Hogwarts-under-construction, with strict Catholicism, not magic, as the reigning principle. The fact that Bobby's father was famous made him as much a target of other students as Harry Potter was in the first book because of his reputation. "Mrs. Kennedy's little boy Bobby," taunted his classmates, and they were right.

At first, Joseph Kennedy did not even know that Bobby was at the priory. His wife made sure of that. Rose had transferred Bobby there, distressed at the Protestant slant of the prep school that Joe had selected for him. She moved Bobby to the intensely religious school before telling Joe anything about it. Just as her parents had steered her away from Wellesley and into a convent school, she guided her chosen son to a school where there were morning and evening prayers, special religious retreats, and Catholic masses four times a week. If his father was going to groom his eldest son for the presidency, Bobby's mother was training her favorite to be a priest.

Bobby liked attending mass, serving as an altar boy,

reciting Latin alone in his room. Devoting himself to service, to God, to the rituals of faith felt exactly right to him. He yearned to belong, to live a moral life, and to serve God. Here, alongside the monks, he found a way, an answer, a path.

Being with the other boys was harder. During Bobby's second year at the priory, his father had been quoted as saying, "Democracy is finished in England. It may be here." Not only was he an appeaser, he was a defeatist who believed some form of dictatorship was inevitable. The backlash against Joseph Kennedy was so intense that he soon resigned the post he had been so honored to receive. As they will, Bobby's schoolmates picked up on their parents' scorn for Kennedy. That only infuriated Joseph's neglected son, who defended his distant, idolized father with his fists. Bobby was all the more on his own. As he said years later, "What I remember most vividly about growing up was going to a lot of different schools, always having to make new friends, and that I was very awkward. . . . I was pretty quiet most of the time. And I didn't mind being alone."

Kids who say they don't mind being alone sometimes mean that they don't think anyone wants them around.

One of his teachers thought, "He didn't look happy, he didn't smile much." Kennedy kept having accidents, injuring himself. And he wasn't doing well in class. His grades were mediocre at best, in the 60s and 70s. By contrast, in 1940 Jack's college thesis was published, and became a best seller. And then the following year, Joseph sold the family home in Bronxville.

An isolated boy is stumbling at school while a brother writes the book everyone is talking about. The home where he had close friends is suddenly taken away by the quiet boy's father, who is both far-off and under attack. A boy under these pressures can become so angry at the world and himself that he becomes self-destructive. Perhaps that was why, in 1941, Bobby joined a cheating ring. Cheating can seem like an effort to do well—as if Bobby were desperate to raise his grades and please his father. But cheating is also a high-risk gamble, a way of inviting adults to catch you, to notice you, to save you. Someone got a copy of a final exam and shared it. Whether Bobby was at the center of the plot or was just carried along is not clear. But he did use the stolen test, and was caught.

A chauffeur arrived in a black limousine and

whisked Bobby away. A place was found for him at Milton Academy, and no one mentioned the scandal out loud—at least not when there were guests in the house to hear.

The Kennedy clan cleaned up its own mistakes. Nothing was to leak out to the world. Bobby's trouble at school was just one of many secrets the family was doing its best to manage. Rosemary, the oldest girl, had long experienced severe emotional problems, which got worse as she aged. In 1941 Joseph agreed to let doctors try an operation in which part of her brain was removed, in the hope that it would diminish her outbursts. The lobotomy left her so damaged she had to be sent away to an institution. Joseph handled this with such secrecy that Rose never knew exactly what had happened to her own daughter.

Rosemary's macabre fate was not even the most troubling story the family had to keep quiet. Joseph Kennedy was a compulsive womanizer. While most of his affairs were brief, he became so involved with the film star Gloria Swanson that he brought her to the family's summer home in Hyannis Port. His pursuit of women was blatant and consuming. That left his children no choice but to reject him entirely, or treat his compulsion as a fact of life. Some even became his accomplices, putting out the word for him so that he could more easily find companions. In turn Rose became all the more the distant, efficient organizer who controlled her territory, her chosen children, and left Joseph to his own devices. The father's obsession poisoned the whole family.

When Bobby was sinking at Portsmouth Priory, he probably did not yet know about Rosemary, or his father's affairs. But what he did not consciously know, he may well have felt: the family had secrets that were never to be spoken. And now he had added one more. The family would protect him. He would not suffer in the outside world. But he was sealed into the silence.

Other wealthy families surely did as much as the Kennedys to hush up their own scandals. But the Kennedys rose just at the moment when the world of publicity—the press, radio, soon television—blossomed. Anytime they needed to protect or advance the family, they found a way to shape what the public would learn. They mastered the arts of "spin" and media manipulation just when these became crucial to political success. Dealing with Bobby's cheating and whisking him off to another school was just one small way in which the well-oiled family machine worked to protect one of its own.

Picture a thin, wiry, short teenager who is so shy he walks four feet behind a girl he is escorting home from chapel. Head down, hands jammed into his pockets, he looks to her like "a bird in a storm." That was one Bobby Kennedy at Milton Academy. But that same boy had been a second-string halfback at Portsmouth Priory, and now, out on the football field, he was a demon, a terror. He was not big for his age or especially fast, but he had strong arms because he worked and worked at it. There was no such thing as "practice" for Bobby. He was as likely to get hurt smashing into a piece of equipment as into an opposing player. He never stopped.

Bobby was now a starter on the varsity. Some of the kids found him weird for being so single-minded. One schoolmate remembered that "Bobby certainly tried hard. He showed absolute determination; he decided to do something, he just gave it everything he had." Even in those appreciative words you can hear the hesitation: "certainly" he "tried"—but all the effort showed him to be uncomfortable, out of place, on his own strange track.

The funny thing is that Bobby's very discomfort, his oddness, drew the attention of the most important student in the whole school. Life at Milton revolved around one young man who was a spectacular natural athlete and completely at ease with himself. David Hackett's charm, his grace under pressure, could disarm even the sternest headmaster and dazzle every fellow student. In fact there is a whole book written about him: *A Separate Peace*, by John Knowles, where he appears as Phineas, the wonder boy. The amazing David Hackett did not need to fit in.

David took a liking to the intense young man who held nothing back on the football field, and who was as irreverent as he was. And perhaps in David, Bobby found someone a bit like his older brothers, but in his own world. With David at Milton, Bobby could be in the circle of the star as he was in the circle of the family: not at the center, but close by, and driving himself without mercy.

Bobby out in front of David, blocking for him; Bobby racing downfield to catch one of David's passes finally drew his father's attention. The very first time Joseph ever praised Bobby to the rest of the family came after he "played a whale of a game."

One reason for Bobby's success in football was that Joe had patiently and carefully taught his brother how to catch and throw, with each pass just a little harder so that Bobby could get used to the speed and sting. Jack's connection to Bobby came through books. At times he shared the adventure stories he was reading with his younger brother. Jack's stories and Joe's games gave Bobby a path to follow: he could admire his older brothers from afar, as if they were the knights and heroes of legend, while trying to emulate them in his own world of schoolboy sports. But in the 1930s a much bloodier form of competition was looming, as Europe stumbled toward a second world war. The war changed everything.

Chapter

★ 3 ★

AS EUROPE PLUNGED into war, Joe and Jack knew exactly what they needed to do. Leaders lead, and if the Kennedy sons aspired to be great statesmen, they would first have to show that they were great soldiers. If men were going to risk their lives, nothing could stop Joe and Jack from being out there with them, in the most dangerous spots—even if they had to cheat to get there.

Joe and Jack both enlisted before Pearl Harbor, but Jack should never have been allowed to serve. Since the mid-thirties he had been battling a persistent stomach problem that even long visits to the Mayo Clinic, one of the most famous medical facilities in the country, could neither diagnose nor cure. In fact, it is possible that the treatments doctors tried may have contributed to the severe back problems for which he was hospitalized in 1940. With these debilitating ailments, he failed physicals for both army and navy officer-candidate schools. But the family pulled strings for Jack. A friend of his father's with an important post in the navy accepted a medical report that downplayed Jack's problems.

Jack was the first to have a chance to show his mettle. On a pitch-black night, the PT (patrol-torpedo) boat on which he was captain was sliced in two by a Japanese destroyer. Keeping absolutely cool and clearheaded, he gathered the survivors and led them on a long swim to a nearby island. That would have been enough to show leadership and courage. But as he was swimming, Jack was carrying the most severely injured crewman on his back, holding him in place by clutching the weakened man's jacket straps in his teeth. Though he was completely exhausted, he swam out again, hoping to signal a friendly ship, and only barely made it back to the island alive. Eventually, after seven days, Kennedy and the nine men he saved, protected, and then held together as a group were rescued.

Jack was a true hero.

The rich man's son who did everything possible to help his men stood for the best in America. Never one to miss a chance to promote his sons, Joseph took every opportunity to publicize Jack's heroism. There was just one person who could not easily join in the shouting.

Perhaps for the first time in his life, Joe was beaten by his younger brother. The sun of praise, of glory, shone on Jack. Quite probably Joe felt he had to match, and even surpass, Jack's achievement. He volunteered for a nearly suicidal mission, piloting a plane filled with 21,170 pounds of high explosives, with the idea that he would parachute out after guiding it into position to destroy a Nazi rocket launcher. The ammunition was so volatile that even signals from radar could set if off. The Americans duly told all of their operators to go silent when Joe took off. But they forgot to pass the instruction on to the English. The Liberator bomber piloted by Joseph Patrick Kennedy Jr. blew up over the English Channel.

The family mourned and moved on. Rose had her faith to guide her. And however emotionally devastated Joseph was, he was a practical man. He intended his son to be the first Catholic president. If that couldn't be Joe, it would be Jack, the hero of PT-109. But where did that leave Bobby?

Bobby was tough—you don't hurl yourself into cold waters or grim-faced defensive linemen if you can't overcome fear. And yet, throughout his life, there was something childlike about him. How many adults still stick out their tongues, or make faces, when they are unhappy? How many hardened politicians, in the midst of desperate campaigns, end their long days with heaping bowls of ice cream? Bobby did, and these were not just eccentricities. Despite his leathery hide he still had a boyish aspect. In fact, the two sides of his personality were connected. He was tougher than most exactly as he was more childlike than most. He was on his own odd course in life, sometimes hard as nails, sometimes his mother's "little pet." But it took time for the family to see that. Compared to the men of Joe and Jack's ilk, he seemed to be nothing at all.

On January 27, 1944, the Red Army, the soldiers of the Soviet Union, finally lifted the siege of Leningrad—a two-year battle that cost over 640,000 Russian lives and was a turning point in the war. On June 6, 1944, D-day, 155,000 Allied soldiers landed in Normandy. Nine days later American planes bombed Japan for the first time. But despite his enlisting in the navy in 1943, Bobby was not going off to war. He had been accepted into Harvard, and in fall of 1944 he entered with the freshman class. That was one delay to serving in battle. Then, even though he was eager to get into the action, the family insisted that he enter officer training. "I wish to hell," he wrote David Hackett, "people would have let me alone to do as I wished, but I suppose I simply must be an officer."

Writing to his close friend, Bobby sounded as protected and out-of-touch as an aristocrat in an English novel. Yet in an earlier note to David he preened with the bravado of a middle-school boy: "Next to John F. Kennedy and J. P. [Joe] Kennedy I'm the toughest

Bobby joined the navy, in December of 1943. He was eighteen, but looked strikingly young. Jack's heroism in the war and Joe Jr.'s death only reinforced Bobby's sense that he was still a boy.

Irishman that lives which makes me the toughest man that lives."

In 1945, Bobby finally managed to get himself aboard a ship—the *Joseph P. Kennedy, Jr.,* named in honor of his brother. But by the time the destroyer sailed, it was the winter of 1946. World War II was over, and Bobby had missed the action. The following spring he was discharged from duty and returned to Harvard. The great cause that defined the men and women of his generation, which took the life of one brother and made a hero of another, only emphasized that Bobby was still a child. But with the war over, Joseph had plans for Jack. He did not have time to wait for Bobby to grow up.

* * *

In even-numbered years there are elections, and as 1946 approached, it was time for a Kennedy to face the voters. Jack was interested, but that was not the main reason why he ran for Congress. As he explained to a friend, "It was like being drafted. My father wanted his eldest son in politics. 'Wanted' isn't the right word. He demanded it."

Politics was the family business, and it was Jack's turn to learn the ropes. But there was a problem: for all of his war-hero record and movie-star looks, Jack was not a natural candidate, at least for a traditional Boston campaign.

As the son of P. J. Kennedy and the son-in-law of Honey Fitz, Joseph knew exactly how Irish candidates were elected in Boston. Campaigning in Irish neighborhoods was all about warmth and charm, being likable and familiar. Honey was famous for perfecting the Irish "switch," which was the ability to shake one voter's hand while smiling at a second and making a third feel important. At any moment, Fitz could be persuaded to use his wonderful voice to sing a sentimental song, reminding voters of their common Irish roots. As a person and a candidate, Jack was the exact opposite of his grandfather.

The Harvard-educated son of a multimillionaire, Jack had little in common with most Irish voters. He had a tense, pinched speaking voice, and sounded stiff giving speeches. Jack was not sure of himself, feeling that he was filling in for Joe, who should have been the chosen one. His self-doubt made him seem all the more awkward and uncomfortable. The last thing he needed in the campaign was his younger brother: "I can't see that sober, silent face breathing new vigor into the ranks," Jack insisted. Instead, he asked a friend to entertain Bobby as he would a child: "You take Bobby out to movies or whatever you two want to do."

Jack underestimated his brother, who was farmed out to seek votes in unlikely places, tough districts where Jack's wealth and style would be particularly unpopular. This turned out to be the perfect challenge for Bobby.

Bobby knew what it was like to be taken for granted. He especially understood the world from a child's point of view. Sports were as important to him as they were to any boy he passed in a school yard. So he came up with the idea of playing softball with neighborhood kids near the local Democratic party headquarters. Even though the ballplayers couldn't vote, they would spread the word that the Kennedys were regular guys. Jack did not carry the areas in which his brother worked, but he did better than expected. Completely on his own, Bobby had found a way to merge his sympathy for children, for outsiders, with the practical necessities of politics. In this small way, he gave a hint of what a tough, determined, and loyal election worker he could be.

Elections were perfect for Bobby. They were like

The Kennedy family moved on after Joe Jr. died. In this 1948 photo, Jack is on the left, next to his sister Jean, their mother Rose, father Joseph, sister Pat, Bobby, sister Eunice, with Ted, the youngest brother, in front.

sports—a great game, with an enemy to defeat and a victory to be won. They were like religion—a ritual in which he could organize the faithful and fight for good. They were like the family dinner table discussions—only now, instead of being silent while his brothers spoke brilliantly, he could join in by helping out. If Jack was learning the family business of running for office, Bobby devoted his apprenticeship to finding innovative ways to run a campaign.

He had good teachers. Typically, one came from sports, another from the family.

At five ten, one hundred and fifty-five pounds, Bobby was small for college football. Full-grown men who had served in the army were now returning to college, giving Harvard the best team it had ever enjoyed. But Bobby worked so hard, and was such a fearless player, that he made the team. The team captain, Kenneth O'Donnell, was Irish and from Massachusetts, but O'Donnell did not like the Kennedys. He disagreed with Joseph's conservative and isolationist politics, and was not impressed by their wealth. Still Bobby caught his eye. "If you were blocking Bobby, you'd knock him down, he'd be up again going after the play. He never let up." Bobby found a circle of friends among athletes like O'Donnell, and shaped his college personality around them: he was the athlete, the tough Irishman, the moxie fighter who would take on anyone. In turn, O'Donnell went on to be one of the Kennedy family's best campaign organizers.

Even as Bobby was playing the hard-bitten jock, he was always looking over his shoulder, checking for signs that his father was noticing and approving. Joseph had his own sharp sense of how to win an election.

"We're going to sell Jack like soap flakes," Joseph announced. Crass as Joseph's plan sounds, it was also very smart. The canny businessman recognized that spending money on advertising and on the media was the political wave of the future. Even without his father's checkbook, though, Jack was speaking to a new kind of voter.

The men and women who served in World War II had seen hell. Whether they were among the liberators of concentration camps who came upon the living skeletons, the troops who landed in the murderous gunfire on D-day, or survivors of the grim and bloody Pacific campaign that ended with two nuclear explosions, returning veterans were shaped by their experiences. After the war, many wanted to pull their lives together by going to college, getting married, starting families. But they also wanted straight-talking leaders who would get things done, not hacks who sang sentimental songs and recycled old, prewar slogans. In 1946, when Jack Kennedy ran for a seat in Congress, it was as the voice of these "New Men."

Jack ran, and he won. Daddy's money + a new appeal + a well-organized campaign, helped just a bit by Bobby's blend of boyish sports and electioneering, were the start. Joseph's dream of crowning a son as president was one step closer to reality.

Jack was a youthful, handsome new candidate, running a new kind of campaign, appealing to voters seeking a new approach. And yet Jack was also a son running at his father's command, with his father's money, to fulfill his father's dream. And Bobby was tagging along behind, trying to prove himself to both his brother and his father.

Chapter

★ 4 ★

WITH JACK LAUNCHED on his political career, Bobby was left on his own to define his future. His college grades were again mediocre, and he barely made it into law school at the University of Virginia. Now set in his personality as the athlete, the tough guy, he enjoyed flouting the gracious, gentlemanly tone of the school. Eating meat with his hands and stomping around his room in his cleats, he was inviting his classmates to see him as rude, daring them to dislike him. He was spoiling for a fight, and in his third year at Virginia he found a worthy one.

Bobby had graduated from Harvard in 1948, the year after Jackie Robinson integrated major-league baseball. Athletics was one public way in which two Americas, the land of white dominance and the land that took its stand against the Nazis, were clashing. During Kennedy's years at Harvard, the football team had one black player, a tackle. At the time, colleges in the South were strictly segregated, and not a single Southern white team ever played against a black player. When Harvard came to play Virginia, the school balked, and insisted on exiling the tackle to a separate house. Kennedy and the rest of his teammates refused to accept those terms. Not only did the team stay together, they played together—the very first time an integrated team appeared in a college football game in the South.

The 1948 Harvard football team, with Bobby wearing number 86. Number 22 is Ken O'Donnell, who brought Bobby into Jack's campaign for the Senate four years later. In 1947 the team had insisted that Chester Pierce, number 70, play with them in a game against Virginia—which was the very first step in integrating sports in the South.

A few years later, in his final year at Virginia, Kennedy was president of the Student Legal Forum, which put him in charge of inviting speakers to come to the school. The same policy of strict segregation that he had opposed as a football player also applied to seating at school events. Kennedy invited a speaker who posed a direct challenge to this policy.

Ralph Bunche was one of the most prominent African Americans of his time. The grandson of a slave, he had earned a doctorate at Harvard. He won the Nobel Peace Prize for his work negotiating between the new state of Israel and its Arab enemies, and was greeted in New York with a ticker tape parade. Ralph Bunche's stand against segregation was clear and absolute.

Even though the rule requiring segregated seating was a Virginia state law, Kennedy and his colleagues on the Student Legal Forum objected. Pushed by the students, the dean of the law school found a way around the state requirement. Dr. Bunche came and spoke to a fully integrated audience.

Bobby's plunge into challenging segregation paid off. At the same time, he was taking another major step in his own life. Although he was the seventh child, in 1950 Bobby became the first of his generation to marry. In Ethel Skakel he found a lively, athletic Catholic woman whose energy matched his own. What is more, she fervently believed in him. Marrying Ethel and starting a family seemed to offer the very best salve for all of his loneliness. Now he was the center of a new family, not an outsider yearning to be included with his father and brothers. Thirteen months after he was the first to marry, Bobby became the first of the siblings to become a parent. In time, he and Ethel would have eleven children.

After graduating from law school, Bobby left with Ethel for Washington. As ever, his father helped out, putting in a good word that landed him a job working for the Justice Department investigating corruption. Now Bobby's crusading spirit would not merely be used to integrate one lecture, but to help the government expose real criminals. How ironic. There had long been rumors that Joseph had made part of his fortune working with bootleggers and gangsters. Bobby was the son most loyal to his father. While Jack could joke about his father's demands, Bobby couldn't afford to; he just wanted to be included. But now Bobby had the job of exposing men who were similar to his father, and might even have dark links to him. The Kennedy crusade to change the world and the family drama of fathers and sons would be played out together in the nation's capital. But shortly after Bobby began his job, the family pulled him back.

* * *

Nineteen fifty-two was a crucial year for Jack. It was time for the next step in the master plan. Now a relaxed, confident politician, he had won three terms in the House. So he decided to run for the Senate in Massachusetts, taking on Henry Cabot Lodge, Jr.

As the expression went, in "Boston, the home of the bean and the cod, the Lowells talk only to the Cabots, and the Cabots talk only to God." The senator was a perfect product of Cabot breeding, and his namesake grandfather had been publicly contemptuous of the Irish. Just as he had done when he flashed across Nantucket Sound in his boat, Jack was challenging the old colonial families. But the Republican Lodge had been elected twice already, and it looked very much like the war hero General Dwight D. Eisenhower would win the presidency, which would help the whole Republican ticket.

Joseph was eagerly pouring money into the campaign, but Jack resented the intrusion and feared that such openhanded spending could turn voters against him. The candidate was hardly speaking to the man bankrolling the campaign, his own father. Ken O'Donnell, who was now working for Jack, knew what he must do. He approached the one person who had limitless energy and absolute loyalty, the one person who could speak to both Joseph and Jack. But Bobby wasn't convinced. "I'll just screw up," he warned his old teammate. O'Donnell knew better. Perfectly obedient and perfectly fearless, the loyal younger brother and the ruthless hatchet man, Bobby was the ideal manager for a Kennedy election. Six years after he had been treated as a child in his brother's first campaign, Bobby took charge of the family's political fate.

If Jack was to speak to a new generation, the Kennedys had to signal that they were not the old party of Honey Fitz, but a dynamic new force, in tune with their times. The Kennedy campaign set out to build a new party organization, run by Bobby and staffed with young people like themselves.

You are Bobby Kennedy, twenty-six years old, skinny as a rail, working eighteen-hour days creating a new kind of political "machine" that can mow down any opposition. Every political hack from the days of Honey Fitz is kicked out, replaced by eager, organized, detail-oriented young people who report to you. You treat everyone in the campaign the way you treat yourself. Work hard, harder, harder than that, making sure your message, delivered by your people, reaches every single household in the state.

You are Bobby Kennedy, twenty-six years old, skinny as a rail, working eighteen-hour days to help elect your brother to the Senate, and you are sent on a mission. There is some unpleasant business to take of, and you are the man for the job. Paul Dever, the governor of Massachusetts, is nearly twice your age. An old-style politician out of touch with new voters, he is slipping in the polls. With his campaign floundering, Dever wants to join forces with the rising Kennedys. Jack says to cut him loose, but "don't get me involved in it." You, Bobby, are to walk in and tell the governor his political life is over.

Bobby dives in, delivers the death sentence, and takes Dever's screams and curses. Bobby leaves a howling governor in his office, and goes back to work. Jack stays clean.

At first Jack was mad at O'Donnell for contacting his brother, whom he still did not trust. But as Bobby willingly did everything from cutting Dever loose to building a political organization from the ground up, Jack began to change his mind. The brothers were figuring out how they could work together as an unbeatable team. Jack would be out before the public, now ever more charming, bright, sophisticated, at ease. Bobby would do the dirty work behind the scenes. But that also meant that all of the family's skill at image making concentrated on Jack. If Bobby was the more obviously bare-knuckled, steel-eyed brother, it was Jack who had to sit under tanning machines so that he appeared healthier than he actually was.

Jack's campaign called on the strengths of the entire family. Rose and the other Kennedy women joined in with a brilliant contribution of their own. They held a series of thirty-three "teas" all around the state. Rose had been the wife of the ambassador to England, and now she would contact women and invite them to come and meet with her. For women who were accustomed to organizing local events, this was a great thrill. Though Jack would put in an appearance, the events were not labeled as political rallies, which made them all the more appealing to women who were drawn to them as glamorous social occasions.

With Bobby in charge, Joseph stepped back. But he was no less important. There was one part of the cam-

people voted with their emotions, not their minds.

McCarthy had come to realize that fear of Communism was one of the most powerful emotional chords of all, and he was especially popular in Massachusetts. If he came to the state to campaign for Senator Lodge, he was sure to erode Jack's Catholic support and to sway some of the very veterans Kennedy was eager to court. Joseph recognized the threat, and he figured out that a large donation to McCarthy's reelection campaign would encourage him to stay home in Wisconsin and not take part in the Massachusetts race.

Rose held her teas. Bobby did everything from straightening out posters to managing the election efforts in every district. Jack was cool and composed when he faced Senator Lodge in a debate. And Joseph's money kept McCarthy on the sidelines. One hour after the polls closed, for the first time in American history, a computer predicted the result. Based on just 7 percent of the votes, UNIVAC I correctly announced that Dwight D. Eisenhower would lead an electoral landslide. Though Eisenhower easily carried Massachusetts, Jack Kennedy bucked the Republican trend and joined McCarthy in the United States Senate.

Jack did not like McCarthy. Kennedy was a thinker who loved to read and enjoyed discussing ideas. Tail-Gunner Joe was a drinker, a loudmouth, a bully. Jack was a real hero, Joe a braggart and a liar. The rest of the Kennedy family saw matters differently. Joseph agreed with Joe's anti-Communism and recognized his power and popularity. He entertained the senator, who went out on dates with a couple of the Kennedy sisters. But the Kennedy with the deepest bond to McCarthy was Bobby. "I liked him almost immediately," Bobby recalled years later, when that was a very unpopular thing to say.

Bobby was eager to join his father in opposing Communism. Indeed he was a moralist, a man who, in a family less devoted to politics, might well have been a priest. Bobby believed with all the fire in his heart that he could best serve good by fighting evil. Joining McCarthy's anti-Communist crusade seemed the best way to be a warrior for good. Even McCarthy's boorish drinking and bullying might have appealed to Bobby—here was someone out of the same mold as the football players who had been his college friends, a leader who was also a tough outsider. Joseph phoned Joe, and Bobby was given a position as a lawyer working with McCarthy's Senate committee seeking out and exposing Communists.

McCarthy and his chief aide, Roy Cohn, swaggered, accused, and spread fear. In fact they had little or no useful information about Communist spies in America. But just as McCarthy had lied about his war record, he lied about the secret intelligence he claimed to have. Combining bluster with the power of the government, he intimidated individuals, companies, schools, and colleges, and a sick mood of suspicion and fear spread in the country.

Bobby Kennedy did not work with McCarthy and Cohn on their smear campaigns. His assignment was to track down ships that were trading with Communist China. And after just five months, he resigned. Perhaps, as he later claimed, he did not approve of McCarthy's behavior. He could not stand Cohn, who was not only unpleasant but evidently homosexual. With his image of masculine toughness, Bobby was always uncomfortable around anyone known to be attracted to men. But there is another possibility. Joe, Sr. made it his business to know everything important that might affect his sons or his family. There was one

From the moment Bobby arrived in Washington, he realized the power held by F.B.I. director J. Edgar Hoover. Hoover, shown here with Jack and Bobby in 1961, would play an important role in the brothers' lives.

man who knew all of the rumors and secrets in Washington: J. Edgar Hoover. The legendary head of the FBI was in close touch with Joseph. Hoover may have signaled that McCarthy was an erratic man whose days of power were numbered.

We will probably never know if Bobby distanced himself from McCarthy because his father received a timely warning from Hoover. But Hoover would go on to play a crucial role in the lives of both Jack and

Bobby Kennedy. Washington was filled with secrets politicians did not want known. Hoover made it his business to learn them all, to file them carefully, and then to use them to warn off any who would threaten him. He was the hedgehog, the rat, burrowing under the nation's capital, safe in his dark kingdom because of all he knew. But, as we have since learned, he had secrets of his own.

Chapter

★ 5 ★

JOSEPH KENNEDY SAID of Bobby, the son he neglected and ignored, "He resembles me much more than any of the other children." How could that be? Bobby "hates the same way I do," Joseph is reported to have added—though, ever careful, he later denied it.

Bobby hated being a runt. He hated not being able to swim. He hated being late and disappointing his father. He hated losing. He hated evil. Bobby sharpened his hatreds into a fine weapon, and then went into battle.

In the 1930s and '40s, as America first struggled with a terrible economic depression, and then marshaled to win a global war, fighting crime had taken a backseat. It was only the rare crusading journalist or principled district attorney who risked alienating the most powerful men in his area by exposing bribery or corruption. But in the 1950s the nation began to look at itself in a new way, all because of a square box with rabbit ears on top.

In 1946 there were only 17,000 television sets in the whole country. In 1950, 500,000 sets were being sold every month. By 1955 two-thirds of American homes had at least one TV. Television linked the nation together. The first time the country really understood how television changed the entire world of crime and law enforcement came in May of 1950 when Senator Estes Kefauver's Special Committee on Organized Crime in Interstate Commerce began its hearings. TV sets in bars, in hospitals, in offices broadcast the confrontation between gangsters and the government. The public could not stop watching.

Now, when Congress questioned a businessman, labor leader, or gangster who was very powerful in his local community, the whole nation judged him. And it was exactly at this moment that Bobby Kennedy rejoined the Senate Permanent Subcommittee on Investigations. When he was working for the Republican McCarthy, Bobby had been an assistant counsel to the Senate committee the senator led. But now he was the chief counsel, the legal advisor, to the whole committee.

This time seated with the Democrats, Bobby was on the side of McCarthy's enemies. Now he could take on Cohn in the national spotlight.

Cohn threatens one of the Democratic senators, indicating that he and McCarthy have evidence against him and are going "to get him on Monday."

"You can't get away with it, Cohn," Kennedy shoots back, his eyes a portrait of fury. "Don't you make any warnings to us about Democratic senators."

"I'll make any warnings to you that I want to—any time, anywhere," Cohn brags. Then, swinging at Kennedy, he dares him, "Do you want to fight right here?"

Cohn's school-yard dare was an indication that events were spinning out of control for the McCarthy side. Due to televised hearings, McCarthy lost much of his power. By December of 1954, the Senate censured him. Perhaps out of a lingering family loyalty to his father, Jack was the only Democrat who did not vote on the measure.

Bobby's stare-down with Cohn showed Kennedy at his toughest and best. He used his fury masterfully. But sometimes dark anger mastered him, especially at just this time. He got into a bloody fight in a park when some softball players refused to make way for his touch football game. When anyone disagreed with him, he blew up or stormed out. One biographer has called this period Bobby's "days of rage."

No one knows exactly what Bobby was going through. Bobby had no problem making hard political choices, but the McCarthy situation was different. When McCarthy died in 1957, Bobby came to the funeral and stood by the grave, but made sure the press did not report it. As a person, he needed to show that he cared. As a politician, he needed to be invisible. Maybe it hurt Bobby to hide how much McCarthy mattered to him. But there is an even darker and more interesting possibility.

Picture a teenager in his last semester of his senior year. He knows he is heading off for college in the fall, leaving his home and family. He doesn't have to listen to his parents—soon they won't even be near him. But he also feels sad looking at his room, knowing he won't be there, won't be a child anymore. And Mom and Dad are paying the bills. He is independent and dependent, and both make him feel angry—he wants to be gone already, and he wants to be kept at home. He deliberately does something he knows his parents will hate—to defy them, to get them to show they care.

Bobby was like that with his father.

By 1956, he was the father of five children, and he moved into a large home that became the headquarters for his own sprawling family. Though Jack had been a senator for only four years, the family decided that he should try to get on the Democratic ticket as the vice-presidential nominee. Bobby took charge of that campaign. While Jack ultimately did not get the nod, he caught the public's eye. And Bobby had shown his mettle. He could serve his brother's cause as well, or better, than the most experienced politician.

Around the same time, Bobby found a calling working for the Senate Investigations Subcommittee. He pointed the work of the group away from hunting for Communists and toward exposing corruption in unions and the hidden influence of gangsters and organized crime.

In all these ways Bobby was no longer a child, no longer just one cog in the Kennedy clan. And yet his father's money paid for the home, his father's influence had gotten him his start in Washington, his father bankrolled and directed Jack's political career. Bobby was still playing Daddy's game by Daddy's rules.

So Bobby, like that teenager in his senior year, got

into fights with random strangers, and into a really big one with his father.

In 1955, Bobby, the brother with the icy blue eyes, set out to expose powerful people who made deals with criminals. Joseph, the father with the icy blue eyes, was often rumored to be exactly that kind of manipulator. Joseph hated his enemies. Bobby hated his. Could Bobby actually turn on his own father?

During a Christmas visit to his father in 1956, Bobby told him of his intention to expose the mob's hold on large unions. Joseph was furious. The family was already planning to help Jack run for president in four years. Bobby's investigation, Joseph warned, would only annoy the unions and would do no good. According to Bobby's sister Jean, their father was "really, deeply, emotionally opposed."

Do not go there, Joseph seemed to be warning. Do not investigate gangsters, unions, secret influence. There are things you should not see. But Bobby would not stop. For the first time—really the only time—he stood up to his father. He was determined to take his crusade against evil anywhere, no matter what it might reveal or how much it might threaten the family's hopes for Jack.

Bobby had found himself, his own self, as a Senate investigator, and not even Jack's future or his father's rage could take that away. He was just as proud of the home life he was building for his family.

What would be an eleven-year-old boy's ideal fantasy of home? Maybe a huge house painted in ice-cream colors with kids zooming all over the place; zip wires running between trees so you could glide, like a paratrooper, across the yard; endless games, serious games of touch football where adults got into trouble if they didn't try hard enough, but also arm-wrestling contests, push-up contests, any test of skill and strength; boxers and astronauts, pop singers and movie stars wandering in and out every night; horses, ponies, a donkey, geese, pigeons, a flock of goats, maybe a giant turtle or an anteater in the basement—the pool would have to be reserved for the baby sea lion. Hickory Hill, the manor Bobby bought from Jack when Ethel was pregnant with their fifth child, turned into exactly this never-never land.

Bobby loved the high-spirited chaos of the place. Hickory Hill was life just as he wanted it to be: kids, friends, political leaders from around the world, the smartest people in the country, all whizzing around in an endless swirl. Run by Ethel, Bobby's greatest fan, Hickory Hill was where Bobby could be Peter Pan. At home, with Ethel, the kids, the chaos, Bobby felt loved. Yet for visitors, and perhaps the Kennedy children, there was also a *Lord of the Flies* aspect to the revelry.

"The whole idea was to relax in a violent fashion," one old friend of Bobby's noticed. The games were never played "just for fun." Picture that eleven-year-old boy, that Peter Pan, left in charge of a household. Every contest would be a blood sport, a test of much more than muscle strength. "He was always judging you," observed one frequent guest. There was an undertow beneath the hilarity. "We want winners," Joseph's family motto, hung like a sword over every game, every flying football, every dash and race.

An aide who traveled with him said, "Bobby had a cruel streak." Leaving your ever-growing band of children amid constant stimulation and chaos is a form of cruelty. To visitors Hickory Hill was a playland; to the children it was their home.

Hickory Hill was Bobby. In one way it was completely different from Joseph's Hyannis Port—with his strict rules about dinner hour, his condemning "look," his mistresses. But in another sense, it was just the same: a paradise built for the hardy, where everyone had to fend for him- or herself.

Bobby yearned for family, but could only create an experience similar to his own. As in every aspect of his life, Bobby tried hard, harder than anyone else. But, as in almost every aspect of his life, he was trapped in his own past. The only two exceptions were politics and Senate investigations.

Bobby was lucky to arrive in Washington just as the amazing spread of television into American homes launched the new era of Senate hearings. But television was just one way Americans were being knit together. Up until the mid-1950s, Americans did not have good roads to take them from one part of the country to another. Road building had been left to the states, and there was no system of interstate highways. But in 1956, President Eisenhower signed a bill committing the country to creating 41,000 miles of new interstate roadways in the next thirteen years. This was a project to appeal to everyone, especially the men paid to drive trucks. "Teamsters" got their name back when they drove teams of horses to pull loads, but by 1950 they were not horsemen, they were truckers. The better the long highways, the more work for men driving big rigs. New highways were the sign of new times. Bobby's Senate committee had set out to investigate criminals who were infiltrating labor unions. And when they reached the Teamsters Union, they found the mother lode.

In the mid-fifties, a man-to-man duel between good and evil spoke to something in Americans. Broadcast on television, boxing was second only to baseball as America's favorite sport. In 1957, Americans rushed to the movies to see Burt Lancaster and Kirk Douglas shoot it out with the Clanton gang in *Gunfight at the O.K. Corral*. Five years earlier, *High Noon* had won four Oscars, including Best Actor for Gary Cooper. These Westerns led viewers from one tense moment to another, until everything was resolved in a final blaze of gunfire. Americans yearned for an undefeated heavyweight boxing champion like Rocky Marciano, or a marshal who would bring as much clarity to their lives as Gary Cooper did to the old West. Bobby Kennedy set out to be that fighter, and that lawman.

Two men face off, glaring at each other. Though neither is large, they are fit, athletic, proud of how well they take care of themselves. Like two jocks in a locker room, each brags that he can do more push-ups than

the other. Their bodies are coiled springs; it seems either
one might snap any second. But neither will. His eyes
like pinpricks, Jimmy Hoffa, the embattled head of the
Teamsters Union, stares at Bobby Kennedy, counsel
to the Senate Investigations Committee, for three min-
utes, five minutes, his face a portrait of cold hatred. But
Kennedy does not flinch. The ferocious menace he sees
in Hoffa actually relaxes him: he has met evil incar-
nate, and he knows he must defeat it. Kennedy is the
force of all that is good and true, cleansing America of
a man who betrayed everyone who trusted him.

Hoffa had risen through the Teamsters Union by
being a harder worker, and a dirtier fighter, than any
union rival or opposing boss. "Guys that tried to break
me," he said proudly, "get broken up." If making sure
that he won involved deals with Mafia bosses, he didn't
mind. Hoffa believed he was tough enough to make
any alliance, and risk any punishment, and come out
smiling. To Kennedy, Hoffa's attitude, his mob ties,
and his power over the trucking industry were a cancer poisoning American life.

Round by round, Hoffa and Kennedy confronted
each other while the country watched on television.
Yet for all the fury of their conflicts, there was a strange

similarity between the two men. They had the bond of equally matched, and equally committed, enemies. "Hoffa," Kennedy once said, "was my first love." Guys who play tackle football often like a good hit to get the juices flowing. Every time they squared off in a hearing room, Hoffa gave Kennedy that bracing jolt.

Bobby's quest to root out corruption in the Teamsters began even before Hoffa took charge of the union. On a cold December day in Chicago, Kennedy and an accountant named Carmen Bellino, who was particularly skilled at figuring out what people were trying to hide, first began to look into the affairs of the Teamsters Union. At the time, Dave Beck, the president of the union, was one of the most respected labor leaders in the country. But Kennedy soon learned that Beck was stealing from the union, and even from the widow of a close friend. Kennedy exposed his corruption, and Beck was forced out of his job.

Hoffa fed Bobby information about Beck, so that the one man above him in the union would be removed. But when Kennedy turned his attention to Hoffa, he faced a much bigger challenge. Hoffa's crimes were not those of greed. He lived modestly, was devoted to his wife, and never drank or smoked.

Hoffa was all business. But that business was the precise meeting place of the America of roads, schools, homes, and proud flags, and the underworld of gangsters, hit men, enforcers, and bribes. Hoffa forced unions to keep criminals on their payrolls and to funnel money to underworld crime families. Investigating Hoffa meant bringing that hidden world to light. Bobby was not just out to indict one man, he wanted to root out the festering underworld of crime and corruption throughout the nation.

Hoffa was a smart and careful man. He always paid in cash, so there was no record of his expenses. He did not have a personal bank account, so no one could track the flow of his money. He carried a bag of quarters, so he could hold all his important conversations on pay phones. But even as Kennedy and Hoffa slugged it out, a police sergeant in the upstate New York town of Apalachin noticed an unusual number of large black cars with out-of-state license plates, and stopped to investigate. What he found changed everything.

The intrepid police officer stumbled upon the gathering that sixty or so of the very highest mob bosses were accustomed to hold every five years. This had been going on for decades, and no one in law enforcement knew. The gangsters scrambled into the woods to escape the local patrolmen, but the country had been served notice. Well-organized criminal gangs were in touch, and able to work together. Crime was not just a local problem, it was a national crisis. Kennedy and his investigators had already been looking at Hoffa's connections to organized crime. Now they started to investigate the Mafia itself.

In his new campaign against the Mafia, Bobby was again aiming for more than a few convictions. He was turning over rocks to expose the wriggling, slimy creatures underneath to the light of day. Kennedy was as brave questioning gangsters as he had been with Hoffa. One typical exchange pitted him against Salvatore "Sam" Giancana, leader of the Chicago mob. Kennedy asked him if he stuffed the people he had killed into the trunks of cars. Giancana laughed.

Kennedy: Would you tell us anything about your operations or will you just giggle every time I ask you a question?

Giancana: I decline to answer because I honestly believe my answer might tend to incriminate me.

Kennedy: I thought only little girls giggled, Mr. Giancana.

Kennedy turned his hearings into tests of manliness. He was fearless in challenging men known to have killed those they didn't like. But he was also taunting them. He was showing hard, tough men that he was harder and tougher.

Kennedy was equally direct in dealing with callous businessmen. The United Auto Workers had been involved in a long, bitter strike against the Kohler Company in Sheboygan, Wisconsin. The company detested unions, and was determined not to give an inch. But when Kennedy flew to Sheboygan, he understood why the UAW had kept up the strike. His questioning of Lyman Conger, the company lawyer, reflected what he had seen with his own eyes:

Kennedy: You say that the men can put the equipment in the oven, then they can step back and eat their lunch during that period of time. How much time is there then before they have to do some more work?

Conger: From 2 to 5 minutes, depending on the piece.

Kennedy: So you feel they can step back from the oven and take off their mask and have their lunch in 2 to 5 minutes.

Conger: Mr. Kennedy, they have been doing it for 36 years.

Kennedy was furious. The union was fighting for just a thirty-minute lunch break, and the company was insisting on these impossible conditions. The coldhearted lawyer bothered him more than the smirking mob boss. Two years after Kennedy grilled Conger, a government board ruled in favor of the strikers, and awarded them the largest back-pay settlement in American history.

In a period in which Americans began to tackle the underworld of crime, corruption, and business abuses, Kennedy led the way. But by 1959, his time to be the marshal was over. The family had let him loose for a turn as a solo crusader; now they reeled him in. His next challenge was obvious: to serve as his brother's campaign manager, and to elect John F. Kennedy as president.

Chapter
★ 6 ★

"SON, YOU'VE GOT to learn to handle a gun like a man," sneered Lyndon Baines Johnson. Then he folded down his six-foot-three frame to extend a hand to Bobby, who was sprawled at his feet. LBJ, as he was known, was pleased with himself. He had just humiliated the slender young Kennedy and proven which one of them was the real man. Kennedy was visiting Johnson's Texas ranch to talk about the presidential race that was coming the next year, in 1960. Seemingly sociable, LBJ suggested they spend some man-to-man time hunting. When Bobby shot the rifle Johnson lent him, the recoil knocked him down. For LBJ, Bobby at his feet just about said it all.

The future was clear to Johnson, Democratic majority leader of the Senate and the most powerful man in Washington. The country needed an experienced leader, a man with a touch of gray in his hair, to tackle the great challenges of the new decade. The Kennedys should go home and play on Daddy's sailboats. When they were ready to shoot—say after eight years of Johnson presidency—they could try running for president.

LBJ was right—the coming presidential race would separate the men from the boys. But not in the ways he expected. Bobby might not know how to handle a rifle, but he sure knew how to run a campaign. And even the Kennedy brothers' youthfulness was an asset. For as the 1960s began, two very different kinds of global change were taking place at once—one involving established leaders like LBJ, the other centered on young people like the Kennedys with cash in their pockets and new ideas in their heads.

"'Moon' Tracked Going Over U.S.," screamed the headline in the *New York Times* on October 4, 1957. The Soviet Union had successfully launched what the paper was calling a new "moon": Sputnik, the world's first artificial satellite. Newspapers around the world buzzed with the Soviet triumph, which left Americans gasping to catch up. Two years later, Fidel Castro completed his overthrow of the Cuban government and established a pro-Soviet state ninety miles from Florida. The Soviets seemed to be leaping ahead in missiles and science, and making friends with powerful revolutionary leaders. America responded by creating a new department, the Advanced Research Projects Agency (ARPA), to develop new forms of military technology.

In 1959, even as world leaders mapped strategies for potential war, a British sociologist identified a powerful new influence in society: the teenage shopper. The children of the parents who had rushed to start families after World War II were entering the teenage years. The "baby boom" generation was starting to buy things for itself, to choose the music, radios, and clothing it liked. By 1960, America felt the edge of this wave as, for the first time in world history, there were more students enrolled in its colleges than laboring on its farms. The same year a rock 'n' roll group called the Beatles made its first appearance, at a nightclub in Hamburg, Germany.

What was this new decade going to be about: clashes between nations, or between generations? As the Kennedy brothers figured out first, it was both.

From the beginning of the Democratic primaries on, the race for the presidency in 1960 was also a battle between the country as it had been and the nation that was starting to emerge. Jack came across as the candidate of youth, fresh ideas, and what he often called "vigor." Kennedy spoke of new frontiers: America needed to look out to the world where the old colonial empires were dying and many new nations were being born. It must gaze up into space, which was wide open to exploration. The nation needed to see past the barriers and restrictions of the past that kept Catholics out of high office and turned blacks into second-class citizens.

Kennedy offered a vision of a presidency that was smarter, younger, and bolder than the term of the benign and distant Eisenhower. When Kennedy's opponents spoke of their experience, he countered with his intelligence and his knowledge of the whole world. Charming and charismatic, he gave voters the sense that he was the voice of the new America of science and college graduates, an America bright and confident enough to stand up to the Soviet challenge. While true to Kennedy, this image was as carefully advertised, manufactured, and sold as that of any TV show or detergent.

Bobby made sure of that.

The final push to realize Joseph's lifelong dream of having a son as president began, appropriately enough, at his home in Palm Beach, Florida. In December of 1959, Bobby, now officially assigned to manage the campaign, joined Jack there to begin serious planning.

"All right, Jack," Bobby demanded, "what has been done about the campaign?" Working with Jack's staff, Bobby had already made up a file of the key contacts in every state, and had systematically rated the loyalty of potential allies on a scale of one to ten. They had

Bobby's role as chief counsel to the Senate Rackets Investigating Committee was his best chance to act on his own. But by 1959, when this picture was taken, he was about to leave it and go to work for the family, aiming to elect his brother as president.

papered the walls of a Washington office with maps, outlining their strengths and weaknesses in every region of the country. But now that Bobby alone was in charge, all of this preparation looked shoddy. "It's ridiculous that more work hasn't been done," Bobby complained. Jack sighed, turned to a friend, and shrugged off his little brother: "How would you like looking forward to that high whining voice blasting into your ear for the next six months?"

Jack was always the older brother making fun of his too-earnest, too-hardworking, too-driven younger brother. But, at the very same time, he had come to rely on exactly those traits. There were three golden keys to the campaigns Bobby ran: energy, intelligence, and money. Energy: his supply was limitless, and he asked nothing less of everyone who worked with him and for him. Intelligence: the Kennedys were smart, and gathered bright people around them. The campaign was like the restless, relentless competition of Hyannis Port and Hickory Hill, but now all the Kennedys were fighting together for the same goal. Money: Joseph had it, and it was available to be spent on anything, literally anything, that would help Jack win.

With Bobby at the center, this whirlwind, this hurricane of political will rolled on. The Kennedys—with their limitless war chest, their astute use of the media, their youthful, handsome candidate—predicted what politics would become. The family's opponents—first Hubert Humphrey in the Democratic primaries, then Lyndon Johnson at the Democratic convention, and finally Richard Nixon in the election—ran campaigns out of another era, and paid the price.

Being a successful politician in the new America meant knowing how to shape television interviews, not handle shotguns.

The Democratic primaries were the showcase for the Kennedys' new brand of politics. Hubert Humphrey was a senator from Minnesota who cared deeply about Civil Rights. He sincerely identified with the average working man. Run with superhuman energy and drive by Bobby, the Kennedy political organization was often chaotic, but to outsiders it seemed to be a sleek, efficient machine. By contrast, Humphrey's campaigns were proudly "disorganized"—a good-faith effort of amateurs. As Humphrey recognized, he was like "the corner grocer running against a chain store."

Even though Humphrey was from a neighboring state, Kennedy defeated him in Wisconsin. Humphrey could console himself by blaming Kennedy money. The Kennedys flew around the state in their own private airplane while Humphrey rattled along in a bus. One day when a plane flew overhead, he joked, "Come down here, Jack, and play fair." When he was in a less forgiving mood, Humphrey revealed how upset he was by the Kennedy fortune, which seemed to be a perversion of politics as he knew it. "I don't think elections should be bought. . . . American politics are far too important to belong to the money men . . . Kennedy is the spoiled candidate and he and that young, emotional juvenile Bobby are spending with wild abandon. . . . Anyone who gets in the way of papa's pet is going to be destroyed."

Bobby *was* emotional and at times juvenile; Jack *was* gliding on his father's wealth. That was true. But Humphrey was out of step with the times. Since 1960, the cost of elections has risen astronomically, and money is far more important to politics than ever. When Humphrey heard the plane overhead, he was getting a taste of what politics would become. The next contest, though, was in West Virginia, and Humphrey held one great advantage. Not only was the state overwhelmingly Protestant, but many voters had a deep suspicion of Catholics. Here would pay. This could be called fair because everyone knew the rules, and the cash registers were open to all. Humphrey would have bought list placements if he could have, but he simply did not have the money. He spent less in the state overall than Jack paid just for TV ads. Joseph Kennedy's money purchased enough names in the right places to guarantee a landslide victory for Jack. This was dirty, backroom, old-fashioned politics. But the message to the nation was that Jack, a young Catholic, could win—even in West Virginia.

The corner store had no chance against the chain. Yet Kennedy's toughest rival was on the sidelines, still waiting his turn: Lyndon Baines Johnson of Texas. No matter how well Kennedy did in the primaries, Johnson thought that he could use his influence to get the power brokers in the party to give him the nomination. And if all else failed, he knew some of Jack's secrets.

Seeing the momentum for Kennedy, Johnson's team decided to attack Jack's glowing image. They knew that he was not as healthy as he pretended to be, and even managed to find out about his most serious illness. Jack suffered from Addison's disease, an affliction of the adrenal glands that he was successfully treating—but that could be fatal. Having such a chronic health problem ran completely counter to his public face of youth, energy, and strength. An ally of Johnson's tracked down a rumor that Jack had collapsed one day and fallen into a coma, and was only revived because a state trooper was rushed to get him his medicine. On two different occasions a priest had actually been called to his bedside to administer the last rites of a dying man. An ailing Jack Kennedy protected by lies and henchmen scurrying off to revive him with needles and pills was hardly a symbol of a vigorous, idealistic new generation.

When the Johnson camp announced their revelations, Bobby exploded.

First he called a news conference and issued a firm statement that "John F. Kennedy has not, nor has he ever, had an ailment described classically as Addison's disease." Outraged, he attacked the stories coming from the Johnson camp as "malicious and false." Then he brandished a doctor's report that said Jack's health was "superb."

In private he was less polite. As Bobby's best biographer vividly describes it, he "leaned over LBJ's right-hand man and, with fists clenched, hissed, 'You'll get yours.'"

Bobby was lying. Jack did have Addison's disease. Joseph hid stashes of medicine around the country so that his son could have it at hand when he needed it. Jack carried around a little black bag of emergency supplies, and went into a panic once when it was misplaced. Bobby was a lawyer, and careful with words. The family made sure Jack's doctor never tested him for the disease, so that he could not be forced to reveal it. And it was just possible to describe Jack's condition as secondary Addison's disease, so it was technically true that he did not have "an ailment classically described as Addison's disease."

But the simple fact is Bobby lied, lied to the press, and lied in the completely false medical report. Most of all he lied in his outrage, his fury. He was like a teenager caught in a lie. "How could you even say that?" the teenager screams, as Bobby did—even though the obvious answer is, "Because it is true."

Politicians lie. Campaign managers lie—or to use the term we favor today, they "spin." It is their job to shape how the public responds to any single issue so that the larger cause is served. Joe McCarthy was right: in a democracy voters most often make their decisions based on emotions and images rather than deep analyses of complex issues. Even if they truly do aim to serve the public good in the long run, when politicians are caught lying, most will find a way to cover up the worst, confuse the issue, or blame their critics.

Bobby was a politician, a spinner. His manufactured outrage protected his brother's candidacy. In the end, that probably was good for the country. And every other leading politician, of both parties, was just as willing to bend the truth. Bobby made a smart, practical choice. He lied.

All of the mainstream newspapers, TV, and radio stations were willing to play along. No one pressed Bobby, and his fury was what stuck in the public's mind. The Johnson team's revelations left Jack unscathed and instead made them look like vicious mudslingers.

At the convention, Johnson and his aides were disorganized and inefficient. By contrast, Bobby worked without rest, and expected the same of everyone around him. Like a bright and compelling military officer, Bobby would stand in front of his troops every day and half command, half charm them as he outlined their tasks. Bobby made sure that his team knew everything about every single one of the delegates, so that they could accurately predict how he or she would vote. As the first round of balloting drew close, Bobby insisted "we can't miss a trick in the next twelve hours." They didn't.

Jack Kennedy was chosen as the Democrats' nominee for president on the first ballot. That's when his troubles began. Jack invited Johnson to be his vice presidential candidate, and LBJ reluctantly accepted. But then Jack had second thoughts, and tried to take the invitation back. As Jack wavered, Bobby was the messenger shuttling between hotel rooms, speaking for his brother. LBJ would not let Jack out of his offer—and he became Kennedy's vice presidential candidate. And for the rest of his life, LBJ hated Bobby, the whiny-voiced kid who dangled him on a string and humiliated him.

The presidential race between Jack and Richard Nixon, who had been Eisenhower's two-term vice president, marked a turning point in American politics. For the first time in history, the candidates agreed to hold a series of televised debates. Most television sets at the time broadcast in black and white. Nixon wore a light gray suit, which made a fuzzy outline on many sets, while Kennedy's dark suit made him stand out. With bags under his eyes and a five o'clock shadow, Nixon seemed to be tired, haggard, even ill. Kennedy, who actually had serious ailments, was the picture of vitality and health. While radio listeners thought Nixon did better in the first debate, Kennedy was the overwhelming victor with the larger TV audience. The debates taught an enduring lesson: on TV, how you look matters more than what you say.

Kennedy's image was well crafted, but he was more than a pretty face. Just two weeks before the election, Coretta Scott King managed to reach a person close to him. She was five months pregnant, and her husband, Dr. Martin Luther King, was in an Atlanta jail, held on a false charge and liable to be sent away for four months of hard labor. Knowing Southern justice, she rightly feared for his life. Though his closest advisers told him that the risk of losing the white South was too great, Jack phoned Mrs. King and lent his support. Bobby had been against making the call, but he then took the next step himself. He called the judge and found a way to arrange for Dr. King's release on bail.

The Kennedy brothers advertised themselves as young and strong, men of courage who would do the right thing even when it was hard. Starting with Mrs.

tion is so much a matter of rumor and possibility that it could be entirely false. But we do know enough to say that the Kennedys, Joseph and his sons, left a legacy that was directly at odds with itself. They stood for the highest principles and aspirations while they made deals with the most unscrupulous men. This started with the patriarch of the clan, who was determined that a son of his would become president. There was no limit to what he would do to accomplish this. In 1960 he saw his ambition realized when Jack won the election.

One year later, Joseph suffered a stroke that left him paralyzed on his right side and able to make just a few sounds, primarily the word *no.* In a fantasy novel this would have been evidence of a grim trade: a father journeys deep into the darkness so that his son may rise to glory. When he emerges he is the shell of a man, only able to register the horror of what he has seen and done. In real life it was a changing of the guard. The old man's sons fulfilled his fondest dream, but now they had to live it without his help.

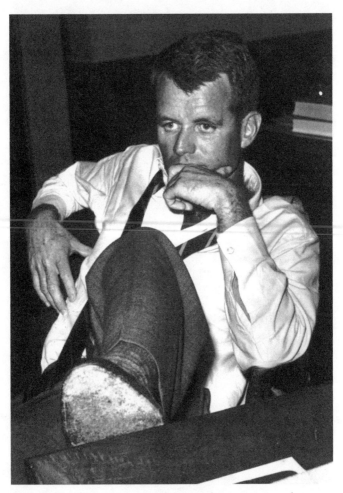

Bobby in his office—the hardworking, tough attorney general.

Chapter

★ 7 ★

JANUARY 20, 1961, was a frigid day in Washington, D.C., as an icy wind blew down its broad avenues. But John F. Kennedy was about to be inaugurated as the youngest president in American history, and that seemed to banish the cold. Marian Anderson, the black singer who had once been banned from singing in a prominent Washington hall by the Daughters of the American Revolution, sang the national anthem. Elected as the voice of a new generation, Kennedy invited Anderson to show the new tone of his administration. Then hatless, defying the wind, his perfect hair in place, he spoke a line that defined his time: "Ask not what your country can do for you—ask what you can do for your country."

Jack was charging the whole nation to live by the ethic Bobby defined for the Kennedy family: "We were to make the effort to be the best." As in the family, all must pull together, and work tirelessly for the common goal. That truly was what Jack and Bobby asked of themselves, which was why the phrase rang true. Jack was telling himself, and all Americans, to take this moment of triumph as an opportunity to make a difference, to be of service.

After helping to elect his brother president, Bobby was not sure what to do next. Jack needed someone in his inner circle who would be absolutely honest with him, and whom he could also completely trust. He offered his brother the job of attorney general. This infuriated critics, as it confirmed their suspicion that the Kennedys were an Irish clan that took care of its own. Bobby actually was an excellent attorney general, but there was something to the criticism. As he soon found out, half of his job was to fight crime, and half to protect his brother.

Jackie Kennedy, the beautiful First Lady, symbolized all that was wonderful about her husband's administration. Thin and stylish, composed and bright, she was everything the many young mothers of the baby boom wished to be. Her clothes, crafted for her by the best American high-fashion designers, were all trim straight lines: absolutely elegant, and perfectly modern. At home in the White House, she and Jack hosted the smartest, most talented people from throughout the world, while all America watched in admiration. When she set out to redecorate the frumpy, neglected home of the presidents, she showed off the tasteful, historically informed makeover on national television.

Jackie and Jack stood for intelligence, grace, and sophistication. The media loved having the golden couple and their two young children to cover, and a glow seemed to radiate from Washington. It was as if the dowdy capital had turned into Camelot, with Arthur and Guinevere reigning over a round table of the best and brightest. That left it to Bobby to battle the nightmare that lurked beneath the kingdom.

Bobby immediately declared a "war on crime"— meaning he was going to continue his mission to expose and cripple the Mafia. But J. Edgar Hoover had no intention of asking his FBI agents to investigate organized crime.

To this day we do not know why Hoover was so resistant to going after the Mafia, and so obsessed with tracking American Communists instead. In New York, four hundred FBI agents spent their days following Communists, and only four investigated gangsters.

And yet the Communist Party in America could only muster a few hundred members, many of whom were actually government agents.

Hoover was a strange man who forbade red neckties, feared germs, and was furious if anyone stepped on his shadow. He lived with his mother until she died, never married, and then lived with a loyal male companion in a home that had many artworks featuring nude images of men. Rumor has it that he came in drag to a homosexual party thrown by Bobby's old enemy Roy Cohn. It is likely that he was attracted to men, and possible—though not proven—that the Mafia had evidence that he was a homosexual, which he would do anything to keep hidden. The Mafia may have been blackmailing him to stay away.

On the other hand, Hoover was a very careful and cautious man, obsessed with maintaining the reputation of the FBI and his position as its head. He may simply have preferred to fight the battles he understood, and resisted being told what to do by an annoying young man like Bobby Kennedy. Especially when Hoover had so much valuable information about Jack.

Ten days after Bobby began his new job, Hoover let him know that he had been gathering files on his brother. This was a way of saying, "Leave me alone, don't threaten me, don't push me. Because if you do, I have enough information to destroy the president."

Joseph Kennedy was such a powerful personality that his children had kept silent about his relentless womanizing. As far as we know, none of them ever confronted him or spoke up for their mother. Sadly, Joseph's compulsion poisoned Jack, who emulated his father by having his own endless string of affairs. Not only did he have extremely frequent involvements before and after his marriage, but he was reckless in the partners he chose. His wartime lover had been photographed with Hitler. As president, he showed equally poor, and potentially damaging, judgment.

Jack's relentless abuse of his marriage was the exact opposite of the Camelot image. Yet neither his enemies nor the press spoke up. Johnson, for example, knew all about Jack's affairs, but had his own record of dalliances and admired Jack for being so successful with women. Even when Johnson's allies spread word about Jack's health, they did not talk openly about his women. According to one congressman, Nixon held off on mentioning the issue because he knew the Kennedys had information about his own girlfriend. Reporters frequently received tips about women Jack had been involved with, but they chose not to print them. The fact that a powerful man had affairs was not, in their view, news. It was just how the world worked.

Bobby himself largely escaped his father's curse. A devout Catholic, devoted to his family, deeply attached to his wife, he was not as driven to pursue women as were his father and brother. He may well have had affairs—endless ink has been spilled on the question of exactly what kind of intimate relationships he and Jack had with the famously sexy film star Marilyn Monroe, with no certain answers. If Bobby was pulled away from his family, it's likely it was to serve his real mistress: work. But Jack's compulsion became Bobby's daily crisis.

Hoover made it clear to Bobby that he knew all about Jack's women and was willing to speak to the press. A lead from the head of the FBI would break the conspiracy of silence and ruin Jack. Even as Bobby set out to investigate the Mafia, he had to negotiate with Hoover. If he were forced to look into the Mafia, Hoover wanted to do it his own way, using wiretaps and "bugs"—electronic ears that could pick up and record conversations.

Approved by the attorney general, FBI men now began to break into homes, bars, and casinos so that they could hide bugging devices. In fact, this evidence was not likely to hold up in court, but it meant that Hoover had access to a whole new layer of secrets.

Bobby agreed to let Hoover use bugging devices to record Giancana's conversations. The electronic surveillance yielded more than Kennedy wanted to know. Apparently in one tape the gangster boasted of contributing to Jack's campaign. Another included information about his involvement in an international plot that remains murky to this day.

Before Castro took power in Cuba, the tropical island was the home of flourishing mob-owned casinos. Castro closed them, which infuriated the Mafia. Even as Bobby was grilling Giancana in the Senate, someone in the Eisenhower government approached the mob boss to use his killers to get rid of Castro. The idea of using the Mafia to kill Castro did not come from Bobby. Still, like Jack, who was a great fan of James Bond, Bobby favored direct action by secret agents licensed to kill. Clearly, if someone had assassinated Castro, Bobby would have been pleased.

Yet a third bug brought the most potentially explosive revelation of all. Judith Exner, a woman Jack saw often, was also involved with both Giancana himself and the great singer Frank Sinatra.

The Kennedys had a taste for being part of the flashbulb world of Hollywood stars and famous entertainers. Pat, one of Bobby's sisters, was married to the actor Peter Lawford, who was part of the "Rat Pack." Essentially playing themselves in the original movie *Ocean's 11*, these were entertainers who flourished in casinos surrounded by showgirls, knocking back hard liquor, and were as comfortable chatting with gangsters as making hit records.

As the voice of government, Bobby was forcefully leading a crackdown on the Mafia. Meanwhile Jack insisted on pursuing beautiful women, which meant that both the Mafia and Hoover had very damaging evidence against him. At the same time, the government was secretly working with the same gangsters in plots against Castro. And then in April of 1961, 1,303 Cuban exiles trained by the Central Intelligence Agency (CIA) invaded their homeland. The world of shadows and secrets exploded into the headlines, and into disaster.

The Bay of Pigs invasion was a complete failure.

The CIA believed that the Cuban people would rise up against Castro. They were wrong. But they also gave the exiles the strong impression that the American government would support them with air cover. The president, though, wanted to disguise America's part in the invasion plan. If he sent airplanes to protect the invaders, that cover story would be blown.

Without American air support, the exile army was trapped between Castro's soldiers and the sea. One hundred fourteen were killed, and 1,189, almost the entire invasion force, surrendered and were put in jail. The CIA had begun planning the attack before Jack took office, and did not work closely with the new administration. Still, it took place after Kennedy was president, and the exiles felt betrayed by the Kennedys. And for Bobby, who hated being seen as weak or cowardly, this was a very personal indictment. It was as if he and his brother had abandoned a friend in a fight. Bobby wanted Castro dead, and he would try anything to make that happen—so long as there was no way to prove he gave the order.

No one is sure precisely how the mob, the plots against Castro, the Kennedy family, and Hoover's men linked together with the crisscrossing strands of women, the Rat Pack, and payoffs from the 1960 election. All of the evidence that seems clear and definitive quickly dissolves into rumors and accusations. But this much is certain: even as the press depicted Washington as a new Camelot, it was abuzz with secrets. Bobby knew many of them, and while much of his time was spent in using that information to fight crime, he was equally obsessed with protecting his brother.

Fighting crime and seeking ways to kill Castro, dealing with Hoover's leaks and Jack's affairs would be enough to test any man. But even as Bobby juggled his secrets, a new crisis was brewing in the American South. A mixed group of black and white civil rights advocates set off from Washington on a Freedom Ride, directly into the lair of the Ku Klux Klan.

Chapter
★ 8 ★

IN 1947, THE Supreme Court had ruled that all buses running between states must be integrated. That same year, a racially mixed group of activists, the first Freedom Riders, tried to put the law into practice in parts of the South. Their courage did not attract much attention. But fourteen years later, with the Kennedys in office, a new alliance of college students belonging to the Student Nonviolent Coordinating Committee (SNCC) and ministers decided to try again. They would put themselves in danger by riding integrated buses through the heart of the segregated South.

Segregation had always been enforced by the threat of white violence. Every daring step taken by the civil rights protesters was a challenge to the bloody rule of the Klan, and they were certain to strike back. Local police and state governments often shared the views of the Klan and other extremists, and even when they did not, they did nothing to challenge their reign of intimidation. When thirteen black and white Freedom Riders set off on two buses in May of 1961, they were daring the Kennedys to stand up for the law and protect them against Southern violence.

Ten days into the trip, the buses reached Anniston, Alabama. Six miles outside of town, a white gang stopped one of the buses. As Hank Thomas, a college-student Freedom Rider, remembers it, "They shot the tires out, and the bus driver was forced to stop. . . . He got off, and man he took off like a rabbit." The bus caught fire and soon exploded, leaving Riders bloody from shattered glass and the blows of the surrounding crowd. But the moment was captured on film, and the burning bus made the nightly TV news. The Riders were vulnerable in Alabama, but they were catching the eyes of the world.

A second bus was boarded by attackers in Anniston, and the two white and two black Riders on it were beaten. Still, the bus made it to Birmingham, whose police chief was a particularly violent racist named Eugene "Bull" Conner. The local Klan had Conner's word that they could have fifteen minutes to do their worst before any police would arrive. The Riders were beaten again, with baseball bats, lead pipes, and bicycle

This photo of the Freedom Ride Bus burning at Anniston, Alabama, tells two stories. It shows the horror and violence of the attack. But the photo itself shocked the world, and helped build support

chains. The wounded Riders fled the city by airplane.

As news from Alabama reached Washington, the president was furious—at the Riders. "Tell them to call it off," he yelled at Harris Wofford, his chief civil rights assistant. Like his brother, Bobby thought the protesters should not have challenged the Klan so directly, and were only meeting with a predictable fate.

Alabama seemed to have defeated the Freedom Rides, as no bus driver was willing to take them farther, and even most of the Riders thought it was suicidal to go on. But Diane Nash, a college student and key member of SNCC, argued that giving up would be a terrible mistake. "We can't let them stop us with violence," she insisted. "If we do, the movement is dead." Three days after Anniston, seven men and three women were ready to ride again, this time starting out from Nashville, if they could find someone to drive them.

Bobby did not share Nash's conviction, but also did not want the law to be flouted. He personally called the Greyhound bus company and insisted that they "had better be getting in touch with Mr. Greyhound or whoever Greyhound is. . . . I am—the Government is—going to be very much upset if this group does not get to continue their trip." He phoned the governor of Alabama to arrange protection for the Riders, and then he sent his assistant John Seigenthaler Sr., a native of Tennessee, down to Nashville to keep watch and report directly to him.

The Riders made it to Birmingham again, defying Bull Conner. They made it from Birmingham to Montgomery, with state troopers flying overhead and escorting them along the highways. But when they arrived in Montgomery, all of their protection disappeared.

Kennedy's aide John Doar was on the phone with him from the Montgomery bus station, and reported what he saw as it happened: "The passengers are coming off. Oh, there are fists, punching. A bunch of men led by a guy with a bleeding face are beating them. There are no cops. It's terrible. It's terrible. There's not a cop in sight. People are yelling 'Get 'em, get 'em.' It's awful."

It was awful. The first person to step off the bus in Montgomery was James Zwerg. A white college student from Wisconsin, he had spent a semester at Fisk, a primarily black university, and had been trained in how to work for change through nonviolent resistance. Inspired by the example of Mohandas Gandhi, who led India to independence through a policy of strict nonviolence, the civil rights protesters were willing to suffer attacks in order to expose the brutality of the segregationists. A man grabbed his bag then hit Zwerg in the face, knocking him down. Zwerg would not fight back, and as he lay there pinned to the ground, the rioters took turns hitting him, breaking his back. A black worker walked by, and could not stand to see the abuse. "Stop beating that kid," he pleaded, "if you want to beat someone, beat me." And they did.

When Seigenthaler saw a female Rider being chased by a woman trying to slug her with a pocketbook, he got out of his car to help her. The Rider warned him off: "Mister, get away. Leave me alone. . . . You're only going to get killed." She was nearly right. He was clubbed from behind and left unconscious on the ground for half an hour. Although FBI agents were present, knew about the attack before it began, and saw the carnage, they did nothing to help.

Bobby could not rely on Hoover, or on the word of the state governor. He sent five hundred federal marshals to take charge. But the confrontation was growing. Martin Luther King had arrived in Montgomery, and he came to the First Baptist Church to hold a rally for the Riders. Fifteen hundred blacks and whites gathered there to listen to King and to support the cause. That made them a perfect target for the racists, who were streaming in for a major showdown. There were just fifty marshals near the church and a crowd of perhaps three thousand angry segregationists. The mob torched a car in front of the church and began to call for burning down the building. As the congregation sang hymns and freedom songs, rocks began to crash through the stained-glass windows. King called Bobby, sounding scared and demanding protection.

Fortunately more of the marshals Bobby had originally sent did arrive, which temporarily eased the crisis. The Riders soon rode on to Mississippi, and Bobby began to understand that they were showing the one virtue he prized above all others: courage. "My God," he said, "they're really fearless, aren't they?"

Like Bobby, college students throughout America admired the courage of the Riders, and no longer felt as cowed by the violence of the racists. In April of the following year a young folksinger wrote a song that captured the feeling of the students who were inspired by the Riders. Bob Dylan's "Blowin' in the Wind" caught the mood of a time of change, when young people could no longer accept the compromises of their parents' world. In 1963, a recording of the song by the trio Peter, Paul and Mary took its place alongside songs about dating, parties, and romance as one of the twenty most popular singles of the year.

The Riders won. When a bus was burned, the whole world saw it. When the police allowed a violent riot, the attorney general stepped in. When a mob threatened a church, it only inspired a growing wave of students to carry on the fight.

There were just thirteen Riders when they first set out, a small group of students challenging the violence of the South. Now the largest generation of college students in American history was starting to rally to their cause, either directly by coming to the South, or indirectly by listening to, buying, and singing songs of protest. The baby boom generation that advertisers had begun to target in 1959 was emerging as a political force.

Bobby was not convinced by the movement. He did not appreciate King's preaching tone. Proud of being a hard-as-nails Irishman, he would never allow himself to show fear, as King did when he called from the First Baptist Church. Unlike the minister, Bobby liked to deal with crises though personal contacts, out of the spotlight, not in public demonstrations. Man to man, Kennedy thought, any two strong, practical leaders could work out a deal.

Bobby and his brother believed in being tough, manly, and private. They mastered the behind-the-scenes maneuvers, nudges, and influence they learned from their father. When the Freedom Riders were in danger, Bobby called the bus company. At the very same time, he was holding private negotiations with the Russian Communists through Georgi Bolshakov, a Soviet colonel he met in Washington. When these personal efforts failed, it very nearly brought about the end of the world.

Chapter

★ 9 ★

"WE HAVE SOME big trouble," Jack warned his brother on the morning of Tuesday, October 16, 1962. "I want you over here."

Experts studying photos taken by a spy plane discovered that the Soviets had placed nuclear missiles on Cuba. Nikita Khrushchev, premier of the Soviet Union, had begun Operation ANADYR, the most dangerous gamble in the entire history of the world. On October 4, a freighter carrying ninety-nine nuclear weapons landed in Cuba. Some were warheads for missiles that could reach the United States; others were nuclear ammunition for battlefield weapons that would be used should the Americans invade. This one ship carried twenty times more explosive power than all the bombs dropped on Germany during World War II.

Khrushchev was planning to dare the Americans by putting nuclear weapons right under their noses.

At one stroke he would change the entire balance of world power. The Soviet leader was determined to force the West to give up the part of Berlin it still controlled—proving to all of Europe who was the dominant power in the region. Now he had the perfect bargaining chip. The Bay of Pigs invasion had showed that the Americans would do anything to get rid of Castro. Now Cuba, the Communist beachhead in the Americas would be safe, protected by nuclear arms.

This would have been a fine plan as long as the Americans did not discover the missiles until they were fully operational. Then it would have been too dangerous for anyone to risk an attack. But the Americans found out before that. What if they bombed the missiles, or invaded Cuba? Khrushchev had made his gamble infinitely riskier by sending battlefield nuclear weapons. This meant that if the Americans sent troops to Cuba, they would be caught up in nuclear combat, and would surely retaliate in kind. Any military action the Americans took was likely to spark a global nuclear war. "Our major problem," the president told his closest advisers, "is the survival of our country . . . without the beginning of the third and perhaps the last war."

When rumors that something unusual was going on in Cuba reached Bobby, he questioned his friend Bolshakov, who assured him that he needn't be concerned. Now the photos showed that Bolshakov had been lying or, at best, misinformed. Furious, Bobby wanted to invade at once. As in his fights with Hoffa and Giancana, his first impulse was to attack, to dive in, to "go in hard."

Jack agreed. "We're going to take out those missiles," the president insisted. Timing was everything. To keep the advantage of surprise, the Americans needed to put on a show. Until they decided what to do, the president and his advisers must pretend that they were completely ignorant of the missiles. If the Soviets so much as counted more limousines than usual at the White House, they might guess that the Americans were calling emergency meetings. That might cause them to speed up their efforts to set up and protect the missiles. The president needed to keep up his normal schedule, as if he did not have a care in the world. In Jack's absence, Bobby became the unofficial leader of the crisis team.

Bobby was in his element. It was exactly like the election campaigns, where Bobby and his aides batted around ideas until late in the night to pick the best strategies. Every key decision maker was heard, every idea considered, and the group neither rushed nor stalled. No ego, no games, just tough, smart guys sharing their ideas, trying to figure out their best move.

On Wednesday the seventeenth, the crisis team began to split into factions: "Hawks," who wanted to bomb or invade at once, and "Doves," who insisted on some form of negotiation. The Hawks had the clock on their side. The longer America delayed, the more enemy missiles would be armed and ready to fire. But every form of military action brought an extremely high risk of setting off a nuclear war.

The best military option was a swift and "surgical" air strike that would take out all of the missiles with only limited casualties. But even the head of the Joint Chiefs of Staff could not guarantee that his airplanes could destroy every missile. If even one nuclear missile fired, an American city could be destroyed. A larger strike backed by an invasion would remove all of the missiles. But surely the Soviets would retaliate against American troops somewhere else in the world. Invading Cuba could solve the missile problem but only by replacing it with an infinitely more devastating world war.

The Hawks had the advantage of recommending strong action that would reinforce America's image as a tough and powerful nation, and the disadvantage of favoring steps likely to kill millions of people. The Doves had the advantage of not suggesting massive death, but the disadvantage of not having any plans that would get the missiles out of Cuba.

By Friday the nineteenth, Jack and Bobby found a way out of the impossible dilemma: you draw a line, and make it absolutely clear to the enemy that if he crosses it, you will do anything to punish him. Anything. The president decided to draw that line, in the sea. He was going to announce a naval blockade, preventing any new weapons from landing in Cuba. This would not eliminate the missiles already on the island, but would show the Soviets that the Americans were determined.

Now it was Bobby's turn. He made the strongest and most eloquent case for announcing a blockade. Though only a summary of his words was taken down, Douglas Dillon, one of the men in the room, recorded his own reactions. Bobby spoke "with intense but quiet passion" and he convinced both Hawks and Doves. Bobby's argument was, Dillon wrote, "a real turning point in history."

Bobby had moved beyond his impulse to attack, and led the way to trying the blockade. Evan Thomas, one of his biographers, sees this switch from a first impulse to pummel an opponent to a softer, more considered response as a key to Bobby's personality. He had labored not to be a weakling, not to be excluded from the glorious world of Kennedy men. That constant effort toughened him, made him love combat, hard football games, angry clashes with strong men. He had developed a callus around his inner, more vulnerable, emotions. But the side of his personality that was formed as his mother's favorite, a boy among sisters, the family man who loved children, was just as real and alive.

The Kennedys were at their very best: two leaders ready to make tough choices, two leaders with the courage and confidence to be patient, two leaders who could encourage the most powerful men in America to speak truthfully, and, together, to arrive at the best decision.

On Monday, October 22, President John F. Kennedy spoke on television to 100 million Americans, then the largest viewing audience in the nation's history. He drew the line by establishing a "quarantine"—no new offensive weapons were to enter Cuba. Then he issued the challenge: if the existing missiles were not removed, America would attack.

Speaking slowly and carefully, in his characteristic Massachusetts/Harvard accent, Kennedy made an extremely firm and clear case. Like a lawyer, he proved that the Soviets had lied about the weapons they were sending to Cuba. Then, like a parent issuing a last and final warning to a child, he explained that any missile fired from Cuba would be treated as a Soviet attack. America would retaliate against the Soviet Union. Though his own father had favored appeasing Hitler, Jack believed the millions of deaths in World War II could have been prevented if the dictator had been confronted early on. As he explained, "The 1930's taught us a clear lesson: aggressive conduct, if allowed to go unchecked and unchallenged, ultimately leads to war."

The crisis that had been unfolding over days was now measured in hours. Twenty-seven ships from the

Soviet Union and its allies were already on their way to Cuba. When the first one reached the quarantine zone, the decision time between world peace and world war would be a matter of minutes, and then seconds.

There were no fax machines at the time, no e-mail, in fact no forms of instant written communication. Letters from the Soviet premier to the president had to be sent in code by telegram to a commercial telegraph office, then taken by messenger to the Soviet embassy, where they would be decoded, translated, and carried to the White House. This could take up to ten hours. Khrushchev's first letter finally reached the president by noon Tuesday, and it was discouraging. He denied that offensive weapons were being sent to Cuba, and refused to hold back any ships. The first Soviet ships would arrive at the quarantine line the next day.

Tuesday evening was a time of grim and fearful anticipation. Jack jotted down a conversation with his brother. Bobby asked, "How does it look?" The president responded, "Ah. Looks like hell—looks real mean, doesn't it?" But they both agreed that they could not back down. If the Soviets felt they could intimidate America, they would do it over and over again.

At this crucial moment, Bobby took things into his own hands. Two journalists he knew had reopened conversations with Bolshakov. Once again there was a private back channel, a way to communicate outside of the spotlight. One of the reporters brought a new offer to the Soviet agent: America would remove the antiquated nuclear-armed Jupiter missiles it had in Turkey in exchange for the Soviets' taking their bombs out of Cuba. According to Soviet records, this idea came directly from "R. Kennedy and his circle." Bobby may have tried to solve the most serious problems through the most unofficial contacts. Even though Bobby told his brother about the meetings with Bolshakov, he apparently did not mention the proposed trade. This nearly had disastrous consequences.

Wednesday morning the American military went on its highest alert just short of actual war: DEFCON 2. The number of nuclear weapons on active status automatically more than doubled, from 1,433 to 2,952. Hundreds of bombers were outfitted with nuclear payloads. Now some decisions were no longer in the hands of the president. Military officers had been trained to follow established guidelines for situations of extreme peril. Any single trigger-happy pilot, any one officer misreading a situation, could set off the war that would destroy human civilization.

The first Soviet ship nearing the quarantine line was being guarded by a submarine, and Soviet submarines often carried nuclear weapons. If the Americans challenged and decided to attack the submarine, the conflict could immediately escalate. The submarine would sink the American ship. The Americans would match that by taking out a Soviet ship. The Soviets would invade Berlin. The Americans would begin shooting down Soviet airplanes. The Soviets would use their missiles. A navy man himself, Jack could all too easily picture the unfolding scenario. As Bobby described it, this was the very worst moment. The president's "hand went up to his face & covered his mouth and he closed his fist. His eyes were tense, almost gray, and we just stared at each other across the table." He "felt we were on the edge of a precipice and it was as if there were no way off."

On the other side of the world, Khrushchev was just as afraid. He had spent the night in his office, sleeping in his clothes. And on Wednesday, Soviet ships began to turn back, respecting the American blockade. The

Americans and Soviets were "eyeball to eyeball," and, as the secretary of state whispered, "the other fellow just blinked."

Not for long. Khrushchev kept changing his mind. On Friday he sent word that he intended to sail his ships straight through to Cuba. But that night, the Soviet premier wrote again, this time in a panic. War would be crazy, suicidal. He offered to remove all of the missiles, if America just guaranteed that it would not invade Cuba.

This was a bargain Kennedy could easily accept, and the crisis might have ended right then. But Khrushchev shifted yet once more. On Saturday he sent a much tougher note, insisting on having the Jupiter missiles removed from Turkey. The idea that Bobby had floated in Washington reached Khrushchev's ear just when he was ready to concede. Knowing that the Americans were willing to give up the Jupiters, Khrushchev could now insist on it.

The remainder of the missile crisis was like the very end of a movie thriller. Bobby went to visit the Soviet ambassador in Washington and insisted the Soviets stick to the terms of Khrushchev's first idea: assurance for Castro in exchange for removing the missiles. America was eventually going to take the missiles out of Turkey. But not now, not as part of a public trade. This was a final offer. And if the Soviets did not make the bargain, war, terrible war, would begin soon.

The Soviet ambassador did listen, and was eager to get word to Moscow. But he was trapped by the communications of the day. There were no direct phone connections between America and the Soviet Union. If he called, he would have had to be passed from one operator to another, any of whom could listen to the conversation. If he sent a teletype message, he would have to type on a special keyboard outfitted for the Cyrillic characters of the Russian alphabet, his words would have to be converted to Roman letters, and the message would have to be routed from Washington to London to Helsinki to Moscow before they were converted back to Cyrillic. He chose the simplest option: he called the telegraph company, and a messenger bicycled to his house to collect the all-important message.

Khrushchev agreed to the deal, and, slowly, the world eased back from the brink of war. The missiles were removed from Cuba, and later Turkey. A hotline was built so that the Soviets and Americans could speak to each other directly and instantaneously. No more bicycle messengers.

In 1964, a study commissioned by the air force mapped out a plan for the ARPANET, an information network that could survive a massive attack. The network would have no center. Instead information would travel among all the connected computers, so that any that survived could communicate as well as they had before the war. When the ARPANET was finally built in 1968, it established the foundation for the Internet. The Cuban Missile Crisis was the height of the Cold War, but in a sense also the beginning of the end of that divided phase of world history. Computers, linkage, the exchange of information was the path of the future, not global domination through ever-more powerful missiles.

The crisis also had mixed meaning for the Kennedy brothers. Jack had his finest moments. He led his country to exactly the right decision by being at once determined and flexible. Bobby shone as well, showing both deep humanity and the courage to deliver the final message so forcefully that the Soviets understood it completely. Sensing each other's needs and opinions, the two brothers worked together so perfectly that they were almost a single force in two different bodies. This was the clan, the family, at its very best.

And yet, Bobby had also muddied the waters with his private efforts. He learned, in the most terrifying manner possible, that doing it by himself, his own way, was not always the right way. At one moment during the crisis, an aide had noticed something different in his office; what was it? "I'm older," Bobby said. He was.

Chapter
★10★

IN 1963, THE Civil Rights Movement came back to challenge the Kennedy brothers again. This time, it was not Bobby who dove into danger. Instead, black people and their white supporters confronted the president and his brother, and demanded that they do more. And while the movement was about rights and laws and fair treatment, it was also about rage.

Rage was what Bobby heard when he invited a small group of black leaders—including the singer Harry Belafonte, the singer-actress Lena Horne, the novelist James Baldwin, and the psychologist Kenneth Clark—to talk to him directly. The group gathered in the Kennedy family apartment in New York. Hour after hour Bobby heard bitter resentment directed at his brother and himself for doing so little while civil rights protesters were putting their lives on the line.

Bobby was the one who had asked to hear from black leaders, and then he was the lightning rod for their anger. He was furious after the New York meeting—as if he'd been sucker punched. He felt that blacks should be grateful for what the Kennedys were doing—which was precisely the attitude Baldwin and the others could not stand. But Bobby was also a smart politician. Even as he fumed, he listened. He recognized that to win the votes of blacks and their white supporters, he could not get by with a Fourth of July speech about equality. He would have to show that he understood black rage.

Something happened to Bobby in that room. Maybe, just maybe, he really did come to identify, to see himself in the fury of people who had been abused, denied their rights, treated as inferiors. But more likely, he was such a good, alert politician that he could put aside his own feelings and listen for a clue to the emotions of black voters. The best boxers learn to ignore the pain of the punches directed at them and instead analyze the strategy of the man who is trying to hurt them. In that way, your toughest opponent is also your best teacher—he exposes your weaknesses. For Bobby, that enemy/guide was Martin Luther King. The next round of their match came in Birmingham, Alabama.

Birmingham was the heart of the segregated South.

Fred Shuttlesworth, a local preacher, paid for his out-spokenness on civil rights when his home was bombed. Yet he survived, and saw a lesson in that. The fight for civil rights, he believed, was a "religious crusade, a fight between light and darkness." That was exactly what Dr. King believed.

The Birmingham campaign was slated to begin in the spring of 1963. Dr. King knew that even if he could not change Birmingham, the public clash would push the Kennedys to do more. King also sensed that black people were tired of waiting. "Bombingham," as it was known, was a test for the whole nation.

This was not what the Kennedy brothers wanted to hear. They had no desire for the country to be swept by a religious crusade against racism, much less to lead it. The Kennedy approach of man-to-man negotiations was the total opposite of King's public demonstrations. Even while in jail, King wrote eloquently about what was really at stake in Birmingham. "Oppressed people cannot remain oppressed forever," he insisted. And black people had reached that breaking point. Either whites would join in with his nonviolent campaign, or the streets of the South would be flowing with blood. Just as the president had warned Khrushchev to remove the missiles from Cuba or face war, King told the South to allow peaceful protest or prepare for violent conflict.

Dr. King's famous "Letter from a Birmingham Jail" spoke for all people of conscience, for "injustice anywhere is a threat to justice everywhere. . . . Whatever affects one directly, affects all indirectly."

Dr. King was saying that the struggle in Birmingham was not a local issue, to be resolved with pragmatic compromises. Instead he spoke with the voice of a prophet. He was not negotiating to improve conditions; he was inspiring everyone, black and white, to live by a higher purpose. If you listened to him, your life changed.

That is, if you could hear him. A prophet sounds like a fraud if you don't believe his words, and Bobby didn't trust King. Take the matter of the Birmingham protests.

King brought schoolchildren, some as young as six years old, into the demonstrations. Police chief Bull Conner did his worst, turning dogs and fire hoses on the young people. This graphic confrontation accomplished exactly what King wanted, exposing the sick violence of the segregationists. TV footage and news photos of the clashes were shocking and helped make the Civil Rights Movement into a national crusade. But Kennedy thought King's use of young people in the marches was a terrible abuse of children.

Typically, the Kennedy brothers worked behind the scenes, using contacts with leading businessmen in Birmingham to win some gains for blacks. But the days in which that kind of negotiation had any chance of settling America's racial problems were over. After yet another set of bombs went off, targeting locations where King had been staying, blacks in the city rioted. As King had predicted, just behind the nonviolent protests was a rage so powerful that people would rather destroy their own neighborhood than continue to live in fear. And once protests tipped into violence, conflicts flared up throughout the country.

It was as if a great gear in the nation ratcheted up a notch. In this heightened atmosphere Bobby started to understand the lessons of that tough meeting in the New York apartment, and to show sympathy for black rage. Even the president shifted his focus from arranging private deals to sharing King's vision of a religious crusade. There was a sound political calculation behind this: the brothers were beginning to believe that the white South would soon be lost anyway, and black votes were crucial for the president. Still, no president since Lincoln had taken moral leadership on civil rights.

When George Wallace, the archsegregationist governor of Alabama, tried to get publicity by personally keeping blacks out of the state university, Bobby sent one of his closest aides to challenge Wallace. The very night of that confrontation, the president went on TV to speak with the nation about civil rights. All of his advisers had told him not to, except Bobby.

Jack spoke of the struggle as a moral crisis in the nation, and announced his support for a bill that would guarantee black rights. But events were moving faster than politics. That same night, Medgar Evers, a leader of the struggle for black rights in Mississippi, was assassinated. Whites had tried to kill Shuttlesworth and King, and now killed Evers. Blacks had destroyed part of Birmingham, and flare-ups were taking place throughout the country. Even as the president committed himself to civil rights, more and more people on both sides of the racial divide turned to violence.

The country was running on two tracks: moving toward a more modern, less segregated society and, at the same time, dividing in ever deeper and more dangerous ways. The Kennedys were directly involved in both strands again over the summer.

On August 28, 1963, speaking at the March on Washington, Martin Luther King gave the speech that defined his life. Addressing the hundreds of thousands of Americans of every hue and background gathered in the plaza in front of the Lincoln Memorial, and the millions who later watched on television, he literally changed the course of American history.

King started out by talking about the promise the nation had made to blacks, a promise that had not been fulfilled. But the crowd wanted more than his prepared words, and he sensed that. In midspeech, he stopped following his script and turned to a thought he'd been exploring in other talks, the idea of a dream.

As he spelled out his dream for America, King caught fire, like a great musician who'd found his line, his melody. Speaking of the future he envisioned for his children, he took not just his audience, but the entire nation with him. He preached the true meaning of America as no one had ever done before. This was not a white politician speaking for the unfortunate, it was a black preacher formulating for all Americans the vision they held in common.

King's great moment at the march was both a high and low mark for Bobby. The Kennedys had been against the rally. But once they knew they could not stop it, they had worked hard, behind the scenes, to make sure it was a success. Bobby planned everything from the route of the march to providing toilets to ensuring that there was a large, racially mixed crowd. A public triumph for King, the march was also, in private, a testament to the Kennedys' skill at organization.

Yet even as Bobby worked to give King the very best platform, he was caught up in a netherworld of spying, wiretapping, and secrets that grew ever more grim. Hoover believed that one of King's closest aides was a Communist agent. Stanley Levinson had once been a member of the party, but had left it years ago. Hoover thought this was just a way to disguise Levinson's deep connection to Moscow. The Kennedy brothers believed the FBI, and did their best to get King to break off contact with his friend and supporter. King was more suspicious of the FBI claim than they, and properly so. Hoover's accusation was most probably an invention or fantasy. But the more King resisted, the more frustrated the Kennedys became. The last thing they needed was to be linked to a black leader who was under the influence of the Communist Party.

As attorney general, Bobby personally had to approve any wiretaps. First he let Hoover spy on Levinson. But then he made an even more disturbing decision. Hoover had new and potentially damaging information about the president and his women: one of his partners was a spy for the Communist East German government. Bobby scrambled to get her out of the country and keep the rumors out of the press. But if Hoover wanted to, he could make life very difficult for Jack just as he was getting ready for the next year's election campaign.

Suspicious of King, annoyed at him for refusing to part company with Levinson, pressed by Hoover, Bobby made a dark choice. He requested a wiretap on King. This idea came from Kennedy, not Hoover. But the results were perfect for the FBI director. For the tap showed that, like the president, King was having his own affairs. Now Hoover set out to blackmail King. Failing that, he sent the tapes directly to Mrs. King, hoping to get her to demand a damaging divorce. But Mrs. King's commitment to the cause was so great that she kept silent. She was as devoted to bringing about change in the country as was her husband. In this she was very like the First Lady, who knew all about her husband's affairs but accepted the president as he was. Hoover did not accomplish anything except to show history his own twisted fear and hatred of King. And Bobby Kennedy left a black mark on his own record.

Bobby's support for the march even as he ordered spying on King was part of the larger story of the two different Americas. One was the land of the "I Have a Dream" speech. This was the America flush with the optimism of the baby boomers, now coming of age. The other was a place of deception, blackmail, and growing violence.

The nation seemed to be stretching as never before toward new ideals, while at the same time, there were disturbing signs that these very goals were just illusions. It was as if America was speeding toward two distinct destinies, and no one knew which would win.

On Wednesday, November 20, Bobby celebrated his thirty-eighth birthday. His brother flew from Washington to Texas the next day to heal a split in the local Democratic Party. On Friday the twenty-second, the president went to Dallas and drove in a motorcade with his wife and the governor of Texas. At 12:30, three shots rang out from the Texas School Book Depository. Half an hour later, John F. Kennedy was dead. It seemed at the time that the race was over. The dark side had won.

After his brother Jack was assassinated, Bobby kept wearing Jack's bomber jacket.

Chapter
★ 11 ★

WHAT DO YOU do when your brother, the president, a person to whom you are bonded so deeply that you and he act as one single being, is shot dead? If you are Bobby Kennedy, you function. You do the right thing. You make sure the president's private files are removed, sealed, protected. You call your mother. You race to comfort Jackie. You organize the funeral. You make sure your shell of a father does not come. You endure the handover of power to the vice president, Lyndon Johnson, a man you despise. You have always performed well with no sleep, getting the job done at any cost. Now you walk, talk, act with no heart, a robot of a man, doing what must be done. Later, sometime much later, you will finally grieve.

One of the first things Bobby said after he heard was, "There's been so much hate." He soon added, "I thought they'd get one of us. . . . I thought it would be me." He had seen the hatred in the Southern whites;

he'd been screamed at by the black intellectuals; he'd been threatened by Hoffa, Giancana, men who were coldhearted killers; he'd plotted against Castro, and knew how deeply the Cuban exiles resented him. He had been fearless, but always knowing that he was walking a very risky path. Now the ground crumbled beneath his feet, taking his brother down.

In Philip Pullman's great fantasy trilogy, His Dark Materials, which begins with *The Golden Compass*, people are invisibly attached to animal daemons, and when the link is severed, they suffer terrible agonies, or die. In a sense Jack and Bobby were that kind of joined being, and in losing Jack, something of Bobby was sheared off. This was literally true in that he was no longer the brother of the president, but a cabinet officer working for a man he hated. But it was also true spiritually, psychologically. Bobby did not know who he was. And what he did know may only have added to his torment.

Bobby had been groomed to be the brother-protector. Every day he fended off Hoover's reports and new political crises, so that Jack could shine. But Jack was killed. On the most basic level, Bobby failed to protect him. Or worse. Lee Harvey Oswald pulled the trigger that killed the president. Oswald had lived in Russia, thought highly of Castro, and read leftist magazines that reported on the plots to kill the Cuban leader. Two days later, on national television, Oswald was shot by Jack Ruby, a man with ties to the underworld. Who was really behind this chain of murders? The official government study, the Warren Commission Report, later concluded that Oswald was a disturbed man, a lone gunman. The report was flawed, and immediately attacked by critics who were certain a larger conspiracy was being covered up. Today, most historians believe that despite its errors, the Warren Commission was right.

But Bobby Kennedy did not believe the lone gunman theory. He hired Walter Sheridan to go deeper, to learn more. Kennedy and Sheridan each told their sons that the full truth about the assassination would never be known. It is possible that Kennedy and Sheridan uncovered key facts that have not been revealed. But that is not the only way to interpret Kennedy's reaction to the assassination.

Sheridan looked deeply into the mob efforts to kill Castro. Eliminating Castro had been Bobby's personal cause, his vendetta. Could it be that he felt responsible for bringing this fate to his brother? Had he risked too much, gone too far in meddling with criminals, with assassination plots? His life mission was to help his brother, to serve his family. Instead, he may have felt that he had opened the door to Jack's destruction. Not only was he severed from a part of himself but he had called down the knife that made the cut.

At the end of that first day, really the morning of the next day, when he was finally alone, someone heard Bobby sob, "Why, God?" That was Bobby's form of prayer. He was trying to make sense of the assassination of his brother, to link this present with the world as it had been just hours before. He made calls, started investigations, tried to figure out who did it, and why. But he didn't just want facts about his brother's killer. He wanted there to be a purpose, a reason, a meaning for this terrible loss. "The innocent suffer," he later wrote. "How can that be possible and God be just?"

Bobby was a religious man and a practical politician. Bobby believed in right and wrong, but he could lie with a sharp tongue and a straight face. Bobby knew his brother's secrets, and yet called him "innocent." Jack's death was the punch Bobby didn't see coming, and it shook him. He needed to find a new way to piece together faith and power, morals and politics. There were no easy answers.

Friends said Bobby looked frail, smaller. Uninterested in his work, he walked alone for hours in wintry fields. Late at night he and Jackie prayed at Jack's grave. Over and over again, he put on the bomber jacket that used to be Jack's, as if he were trying to feel the touch of his brother's skin. One friend thought he was afraid to let go of the pain he felt, for once he did, Jack would be further away, truly gone.

Like her husband, Jackie was well-read. She offered Bobby books, and one in particular showed him a way to emerge from his grim state: Edith Hamilton's *The Greek Way*. Hamilton's book introduced him to the ancient Greeks. The Greeks talked about hubris, the overweening pride of some families, and how that arrogance brings down a punishment from the gods.

The Kennedy clan had flown too high and been singed, burned, by the sun. While painful, this way of seeing Jack's death made sense to Bobby. It was the beginning of an answer to his terrible question, "Why God?" And then he read Hamilton's description of the playwright Aeschylus.

God teaches only through suffering, Aeschylus

wrote. Bobby memorized one passage, and repeated it often: "And even in our sleep pain that cannot forget falls drop by drop upon the heart, and in our own despite, against our will, comes wisdom to us by the awful grace of God." In the silence of the night, in his restless walks, in his empty days, Kennedy was feeling the pain of Jack's loss. Day by day, hour by hour, this was pure torture. But, Aeschylus promised, it could be something more. Only suffering so intense could burn through pride, and etch wisdom on his callused heart.

Hamilton and the ancient Greeks gave Bobby a sober, tragic sense of purpose. Nothing would bring Jack back, or salve the pain of his loss. Bobby would simply have to bear that burden. The family had been arrogant, prideful, and paid the blood price. But there was a path ahead. Abandoned, marooned in life, he still had the chance to reflect, to learn, and to serve.

Chapter
★12★

THE ASSASSINATION OF President Kennedy took place just as many baby boomers hit full adolescence, and established a mood for the decade. The world was new, fiercely so. The world of parents and leaders seemed to be one of oppression, segregation, violence. It was time for a younger generation to take the lead, to make things right. This sense of aggressive, unstoppable newness was not just expressed in politics; more than anything else it was a matter of culture, attitude, and style.

In the fifties, women's fashions focused on well-tailored clothes and beautiful fabrics. The standard hemline was always several inches below the knee. These outfits suited established, married women. In 1964 the London designer Mary Quant raised the hemline on her miniskirts to six or even seven inches above the knee. Since these designs only looked good on younger women, being young and daring meant being fashionable. The same year, "I Want to Hold Your Hand," a Beatles song, became the most popular single in America. The Beatles were not just a talented singing group. They were famous as much for their long hair, London fashions, and the frenzy they inspired in their female fans as for their music. If the early sixties was the time of the Rat Pack, suave adult crooners who were always under control, by 1964 it was the era of Beatlemania: teenage girls screaming at the top of their lungs.

To be young meant to be alive—to new music, to new ways of dressing, to new ideas. All of the separations of the fifties—the Cold War, racial segregation, even the man-to-man clashes of TV Westerns—seemed like the opposite of this youthful energy. John Kennedy had been the symbol of youth and power. Now that he was gone, who could young people believe in? Jackie and her allies in the press worked tirelessly to idealize the slain president as a kind of King Arthur. If Jack himself would never return, they held out the hope that someone, perhaps another Kennedy, could bring back that fabled moment.

Bobby was in mourning, dealing with his own private agonies. Though Johnson went out of his way to be considerate to Bobby, Jackie, and their circle of advisers and friends, something was missing. He and Bobby had been enemies ever since the hunting trip in Texas and the mixed messages of the Democratic convention. In the most painful of ironies, Johnson, a Southerner, a master of old politics, now became the real architect of change.

The poisonous feeling between Kennedy and Johnson went very deep, and worsened over time. The new president was like a strong but deeply suspicious king obsessed with the sense that his son disliked him and was plotting against him; while Kennedy was like a dynamic, popular prince who detests his father and knows the feeling is mutual. About half of what each suspected about the other was true, and the other half insane, yet figuring what was insight and what was paranoia kept their army of aides jumping. Every step either one took to ease the tensions was misread by the other, and only made matters worse.

This cycle of bad blood and suspicion began the moment of the assassination. President Kennedy had been murdered in Texas, Johnson's home state. To Bobby's close circle of supporters and friends, Johnson represented everything vile in the nation. Johnson

President Lyndon Johnson and Bobby hated each other and were deeply suspicious of each other—feelings that are not hard to see in this 1964 photo.

smarted from their contempt. Now that he was president, in a nation eager to honor its slain leader, he had a chance to do great things, and he grasped the opportunity. The fact that he would be carrying Jack's sword, winning his victories, made the battle all the sweeter for Johnson, and more bitter for Bobby.

In 1964, it was Johnson who shepherded Jack Kennedy's civil rights bill through Congress and signed it into law. The Kennedys were eager to support voting rights for blacks in the South. But it was Johnson who, in 1965, initiated, passed, and signed a voting rights bill. That same year he was responsible for another law that made the most far-reaching challenge yet to the America of the Klan and segregationists.

Building on an idea Bobby had first suggested as attorney general, Johnson dismantled the barriers that had severely restricted immigration to America. Since 1924, tiny annual quotas for immigrants from anywhere outside of Northern Europe had effectively kept out all of those would-be Americans. The 1965 law knocked down those barriers. In the following decades, this brought about a fundamental change in the nation's population. Since Johnson's bill became law, the overwhelming majority of new Americans have come from Mexico and Latin America, from Asia, and from the Caribbean. Modern America, in which Hispanics are the largest minority, salsa is more popular than ketchup, and both political parties eagerly court the Asian vote, is Johnson's creation.

Johnson's revolution, for it was that, was built on the moral passion of the Civil Rights Movement. As King had correctly foreseen, once the brave bus riders and marchers challenged the rule of segregation backed by violence, the whole idea that America was fundamentally white, Protestant, and European came into question. Cheered on by an ever-growing cohort of young voters, Johnson did his best to right every wrong in the nation.

Called the Great Society, Johnson's program included Medicare and Medicaid to bring health care to the poor and elderly, higher minimum wages to help the poorest workers, federal money for housing and the hungry, and much more. In his lavish support for schools and libraries, he even inadvertently helped to create young adult literature. Librarians, facing record numbers of teenage readers and flush with money LBJ authorized, created the YA section of the library, which would eventually be filled with books such as *The Outsiders*, *The Pigman*, and *Go Ask Alice*.

The most concrete legacy of John Kennedy's aborted presidency was the group of bills Johnson passed. Yet for Bobby, Johnson's successes poured acid on his emotional wounds. He felt that he and his brother had brought a new spirit of youth, intelligence, and courage to the government. Johnson was part of the old guard, and was only giving form to (and taking credit for) the Kennedys' ideas. To Bobby, it was as if everything precious had been stolen from him.

Bobby's role in the family was changing, too, as Ted, the youngest brother, had been elected to the Senate. Instead of being Jack's shadow, Bobby had become the elder. The large circle of aides who had worked for him or his brother looked to him for leadership. But what should he do? Johnson was certain to be the Democratic Party nominee in 1964, and equally likely to win the election.

In August of 1964, the Democrats were to hold their convention in Atlantic City, New Jersey. The convention was sure to be a good moment for the party, which was favored in all of the polls. Seeing that he would have no part in the national ticket, Kennedy decided to run for the Senate in New York. But he was still slated to make an appearance at the Democratic convention to introduce a film about his slain brother.

On August 27, the crowd responded to Bobby with a passion unlike any ever seen in a convention. When he came out to speak, people began to clap, and clap, and clap. There was no music, no fanfare, no balloons. This was pure emotion. For sixteen solid minutes Bobby Kennedy stood, and the audience poured out its love for him, for his family, for his dead brother.

Bobby gave his planned speech, ending with a few lines from Shakespeare, which Jackie had brought to his attention. He spoke of his brother as Juliet did of Romeo:

When he shall die,
Take him and cut him out in little stars,
And he will make the face of heaven so fine
That all the world will be in love with night,
And pay no worship to the garish sun.

Johnson was the president, a powerful, popular, and effective leader. The convention would enthusiastically support him. But Kennedy was something else. He was a living link with his brother. In the endless clapping, Kennedy heard exactly what he had felt— Johnson might accomplish a great deal, but it was the Kennedys who had changed the nation. Johnson was glaring sun, hogging the sweating daylight. But it was Jack whose martyred body shone through the night and won people's hearts.

Every round of applause rippled toward Bobby saying, "Thank you, thank you for giving us hope" and "Have courage, take heart, see how much you and your brother meant, mean to us." One week after speaking

Vietnam was a small country half a world away from America. When he was a young senator, Jack had admired the toughness and determination of the Vietnamese fighting against the French to have their own government. But by the time he became president, he viewed those fighters, now openly Communists, differently. He and his best advisers believed the nations of the world were dominoes standing on their edge. If the wrong piece fell, it would set off a wave that could reach clear across the planet. The northern half of Vietnam was already Communist. That was bad enough. But even within South Vietnam, there was an active, resourceful group of independence fighters turned into Communist guerilla fighters, the National Liberation Front (NLF). If they succeeded in overthrowing the government, all of Vietnam would be Communist. Once that happened, the rest of Southeast Asia was in danger, which would then pressure India and even the Middle East. As President Kennedy and his advisers saw it, the fate of South Vietnam was the destiny of a good part of the world. But what could America do to hold back the NLF and to shore up South Vietnam?

Jack and Bobby had decided to build a counterinsurgency force that would be an American version of the

NLF: a small set of well-trained, fearless, smart fighters. The Green Berets were created, and the modern Navy Seals were established, to be exactly this kind of special soldier. In effect these secret warriors would be a cadre of Kennedys. They would think on their feet and do whatever was necessary. They would recognize the Vietnamese people's real needs for better government, but would be relentless in battling the Communists. In secret, and with no admission of government involvement, these supersoldiers would clear away the obstructions that were keeping Vietnam trapped in its past. Then a new government would bring reform so that the people's needs were met and they were no longer drawn to Communism.

Each year, President Kennedy had approved sending more money and highly trained military men to Vietnam. But the plan had failed. American advisers and Green Berets were having no success either in improving the South Vietnamese army or delivering key blows to the NLF.

President Kennedy had been left with two bad alternatives. He could pull Americans out of South Vietnam. But as in Cuba after the Bay of Pigs, this meant encouraging the Communists to feel that

America was a paper tiger, easily defeated. He could almost hear the other dominoes in Asia falling. Or he could give up on the strategy of victory through stealth and send in real armies. If North Vietnam could be pummeled into submission, it would have to stop supporting the NLF, which would leave South Vietnam stable and secure. Neither choice had appealed to the president—who was assassinated before he had to make a final decision.

Johnson was a dutiful, responsible government man who, like John Kennedy, believed that the lesson of World War II was that you must stand up to evil. As a result he committed more and more men first to defending South Vietnam, then to a true war against the North. That left it to Bobby to listen to the growing howls of protest against the war, and to agonize over what position to take. The Vietnam War was a legacy of one Kennedy brother, and now it was the defining crisis for another.

Chapter
★ 13 ★

ON AUGUST 11, 1965, a police officer in the Watts section of Los Angeles pulled over a black driver on suspicion of drunken driving. This minor incident quickly escalated as the driver's brother and mother joined in on his side and the officers assaulted the brothers with their batons. An angry crowd gathered, and exploded into violence when the police left. For six days Watts burned, leaving six people dead and one thousand injured. The black fury that had erupted in Birmingham in 1963 was spreading, just as more and more radical leaders preached violent revolution. In the following years there would be riots in 127 cities, with the bloodiest outbreaks in Detroit and Newark. As liberals agonized over the destruction, black militants saluted the flames with a new slogan, "Burn, baby, burn." If President Kennedy had represented the hope of a better nation, the riot-torn cities seemed proof that America was trapped in a nightmare.

Johnson had declared war on poverty, and passed far more civil rights legislation than any president in American history. He could not understand the riots and destruction. But Bobby could. He identified with angry young men who would rather destroy everything than accept the conditions they lived in. Learning of young men who looted burning stores, he saw them as just "kids in trouble" and added, "I got in trouble when I was that age." The family had hushed up his cheating scandal. But Bobby remembered the boy who had to be hustled out of a school in a black limousine. Perhaps in the ravaged cities he felt an echo of his own emotional landscape.

Carried along on these tides of feeling, Bobby came to identify with even the most extreme radicals and revolutionaries. Bobby visited Latin America later in the year and the people chanted "Kennedy" as enthusiastically as did Democratic delegates in Atlantic City. He insisted on visiting the poorest neighborhoods and grimmest mines and responded exactly as he had to the riots in America. If he had grown up in those conditions, he remarked, "I'd be a Communist, too."

Is that true? Would Bobby, son of Joseph the Wall Street mogul, a boy who never had to spend his own money, whose way was paved to Harvard, would he really have been a Communist if he'd been born poor? Or was that just a good line he learned to use? He also said he would have been a revolutionary, that he wished he'd been born an Indian, or in an urban ghetto. Bobby knew how to erase his privileged past and claim a bond with suffering, angry people.

Asking whether Bobby was sincere is like asking whether the sixties protest songs were sincere, or if rap songs are today. Hip-hop artists often talk about "keeping it real." Their clothes, gestures, language all advertise that they are "street." And yet being seen as "real" or "street" also sells music—and as much to kids living comfortable suburban lives as to anyone else. Rap speaks tough, and it sells speaking tough.

Bobby learned to say the right things, in part because angry voices sounded to him like his own. The insightful biographer Evan Thomas believes that when Bobby said he identified with radicals he really meant it. Their extremism spoke to something in him. But the historian Ronald Steel thinks Bobby would have disappointed the "white radicals who found him a 'rebel.'" Steel thinks Bobby might have liked the idea of trying out alternate lives as a Communist, black revolutionary, or poor Indian. But only in the same way as he enjoyed all sorts of adventures, while basically remaining "a Catholic conservative." Bobby was a mouthpiece for views he only partially shared, and that can be very dangerous.

Demagogues who whip up the needs of the desperate are often the most cynical leaders—they would rather let rage loose than tame it. This was all the more true in the sixties, when it was fashionable to be a revolutionary. At its worst, Bobby's effort to show how sympathetic he was to extreme radicals was either cynical or reckless. Either he was playing for votes, or playing with fire.

Still, even if Kennedy sought out society's victims for his own purposes, his involvement was extraordinary. The head of the most powerful political family in America set out on a crusade to serve as the voice of the excluded, the desperate, and the damned.

No one was more vulnerable than the migrant workers of central California. The laborers were Catholic, Spanish-speaking, often illegal, and employed by owners who had the right to send them home at will. In a nation that many still saw as dominantly, and properly, white and Protestant, they were utterly invisible and absolutely powerless.

Under President Kennedy, the government had finally begun to enforce rules protecting workers. At the same time, Cesar Chavez, a devout Catholic who was inspired by Gandhi and the Civil Rights Movement, had started organizing the migrant workers into a union. In March of 1966, Bobby flew to California to meet him.

When he arrived in the fields, Bobby saw what the workers faced and he got angry. He challenged a local officer, who was illegally arresting innocent workers just because they might later riot. "I suggest," he said sardonically, "that the sheriff . . . read the Constitution of the United States." Kennedy and Chavez immediately understood and liked each other. The hardworking, courageous organizer was the senator's ideal man: a person determined to do good who fights against all odds, and who wins. Kennedy found a soul mate in the fiercely determined but soft-spoken Chavez. And the migrant worker, whose family had lost its land in the Depression, who had been bounced through more than thirty schools, who had heard insults and been discriminated against throughout his life, now had a most powerful brother.

Not long after he returned to New York, Kennedy accepted an offer to go to South Africa and speak at the University of Cape Town. After World War II, as most of the world condemned the Nazis' murderous racial theories, South Africa had adopted a new and extremely rigid policy of racial separation in 1948. Called apartheid, it was designed to ensure the permanent dominance of white South Africans. Although black and white South Africans worked to break down this system of racial rule, their fight was slow and discouraging.

Kennedy went to South Africa on his own, not as a representative of the American government—which neither trusted him nor supported his efforts. The very fact that he was there alone challenging a hostile government inspired Kennedy and his speechwriters. "Human history," he declared, "is shaped [by] numberless diverse acts of courage and belief."

Courage and belief were the polestars of Bobby's life.

"Each time a man stands up for an ideal," he went on, "or acts to improve the lot of others, or strikes out against injustice, he sends a tiny ripple of hope." What a striking image: one person's courage sets off ripples. And those waves expand, "crossing each other from a million different centers of energy and daring" until they "build a current which can sweep down the mightiest walls of oppression and resistance."

Kennedy's words echoed King's in his letter from the Birmingham jail, and they captured the best side of all of the protest movements of the sixties, whether in America or South Africa, or in Czechoslovakia—where people demonstrated against the Communists until Soviet tanks silenced them. Individuals, even the most outcast and neglected, began to feel that they had a voice, had a right to be heard, and that they could stand up for themselves.

Kennedy was becoming a symbol of the worldwide movement for change. He walked the streets of a poor black neighborhood in Brooklyn; a squatter's slum in Lima, Peru; a migrant worker camp in Delano, California; a township in South Africa so neglected by the government it did not even have a fire station. Everywhere he went, he wanted to understand the needs of the people he met, the victims of societies that ignored or abused them. It was this phase of his life that, to his

Bobby was known for liking children and connecting with them. Here he is in the Bedford-Stuyvesant neighborhood in Brooklyn, in 1966.

admirers, made him a kind of modern-day Jesus. He sought out the poor and outcast, and made their cause his own. Kennedy's supporters were liberals, and being seen in all of these locations only made him shine all the more brightly in their eyes. But the trips were not "photo ops" dreamed up by public relations experts.

Kennedy came alive in these visits because he craved the contact himself. He understood people aching with need; people suffering, neglected by the wealthy and the powerful. Their extreme lives were like his extreme emotions: his rage, his grief, his drive to battle the world.

If there was one politician in America who might actually understand and be able to reach the radicals who were preaching revolution, it was Bobby Kennedy. But, more and more, the cause that was capturing the attention of militants, of college students, even of liberals, was Vietnam. The fighting in Vietnam became the symbol for everything that was wrong with American society. The war in Vietnam seemed like the America of violence and racism incarnate.

By law, eighteen-year-old males were eligible to be drafted into military service. One hundred thousand were called in 1964, and that number quadrupled the following year, when President Johnson committed American troops to the fighting. Vietnam was the issue on the minds of all young Americans. And yet, Bobby did not come out against the war. Deciding what to say about the Vietnam War was the most painful and difficult choice of his life.

Bobby was in a political trap, and the more he pulled and twisted to get out of his bind, the worse it got. He knew that Johnson was watching his every move and statement. Even the smallest sign that he disapproved of the president's policies would be taken as a declaration of political war, the opening round of a contest for control of the Democratic Party. Believing that Kennedy was openly defying him would only push Johnson to commit more money and men to the war. And the president would use his considerable power and skill to attack Kennedy. Bobby had seen that already.

LBJ warned Bobby directly that if he saw the slightest hint that Kennedy was undermining his Vietnam policy, he would "destroy you and every one of your dove friends." He meant it. From the moment he took office, LBJ formed the friendliest of bonds with Hoover. The head of the FBI had many juicy tidbits in his files and was eager to share them with Johnson. Hoover knew that Bobby had approved wiretaps and bugs, including the one on King. He knew that Kennedy had been at the center of plotting to kill Castro. The cold, amoral attorney general who would spy on the leader of the Civil Rights Movement and plot against a leftist hero was the opposite of the image Kennedy now presented to the public. Every time Johnson thought it would suit him, he would leak yet another bit of information about Kennedy to a friendly columnist, and Bobby's poll ratings would plummet.

Hoover's files were the sword Johnson held over Bobby's head to keep him in line. But leaks actually did just the opposite. Every time Johnson passed along some dirt, Kennedy had less reason to keep silent. The more his supporters knew about his grim past, the more important it was for him to show that he was now a different man.

There was no room for Kennedy to waver: either he had to be a complete Johnson loyalist, or an out-and-out rebel. And as he weighed his choices, the 1968 election drew closer. Was he willing to split his party? Run against the president in the primaries? Kennedy was a realist who understood party politics. He was a clan loyalist, who knew how damaging it could be to break ranks. But he also knew the war was wrong and getting worse. The stand he took on Vietnam would define his political future.

* * *

In 1967, nine thousand Americans were killed in Vietnam, and another sixty thousand were wounded. This bloody war was costing over $2 billion a month and seemed no closer to an end. President Johnson's approval ratings hit an all-time low of 39 percent in August. As the shadow of the war darkened, there was one question Bobby and his supporters had to answer, and could not answer: Who is Bobby Kennedy?

Was Kennedy a priest in politician's clothing? He traveled to Mississippi to see the poorest of black sharecroppers and was sickened, devastated by what he found. In a small wooden shack with no windows, he came upon a child suffering from malnutrition, staring blankly into space. In tears, Kennedy could not stand to see such neglect. Furious at the thought that the richest nation in the world was so abusing and ignoring its own children, he rushed from one official to another to get food aid to the families. He visited American Indians, who, for centuries, had had their land stolen and their religion suppressed by greedy or insensitive governments. He responded to the suffering, the needs, of outcasts like a man who had found his calling.

Or was he a politician in priest's clothing? He gathered groups of aides to meet in secret to debate his future. Should he run against Johnson? Ever alert to polls, to the advice of political experts, he was testing the waters, weighing out what would be his best move. These were the actions of the most calculating and savvy politician.

To make it worse, another candidate, the poet and senator Eugene McCarthy (no relation of Joe's), was already in the race as the standard-bearer for Democrats who were determined to end the war. Idealistic college students admired McCarthy for entering on principle, not hesitating and weighing the odds. To join in the race after McCarthy made Bobby seem like a spoilsport. But to stay on the sidelines meant effectively giving up his role in the Democratic Party.

Now the father of ten children (with another on the way), Kennedy was the head of two families—his own and Jack's. Running for president meant putting himself in the sights of any crazed killer. His loyal brother Ted did not want him to take any risks. Though his father could no longer talk or write, Bobby knew that Joseph would agree with Ted: his place was to lead and protect the family.

The very first time Bobby stood up in the Senate

and expressed hesitation about the war in Vietnam, he began by admitting that it was he, and his brother, who first involved American forces in that conflict. To run for president, and to do so as the voice of those against the war, was to run against Jack's legacy. It was the most public announcement possible that the great brother, the hero, the martyred King Arthur, had been wrong.

Priest, politician, father, clan leader, brother-protector: Bobby was all of these, and one thing more. There was one more character trait he kept seeing in the mirror, and it was the one that he could not stand. When he came to give a speech at New York's liberal Brooklyn College, a student hung a banner reading, "Hawk, Dove—or Chicken?" The one thing Bobby could never accept was cowardice. More than any-thing else, he believed a man must accept his destiny and do the right thing. While every sane, rational, cal-culating, or familial argument told him to stay out of the presidential race, to leave Johnson to face his own failures in Vietnam, another voice told him he was be-ing a coward. For a man whose motto might have been "Courage Before All," this was the worst indictment.

January 1968: the ten thousandth American airplane was shot down over Vietnam, and Bobby Kennedy reached a decision. He told the press that he was not going to run against Johnson for the Democratic nomination. He chose his familiar behind-the-scenes role, his place in the family, his sanest calculation, leaving the nation to wrestle with the war without his leadership. Sealed off in his own gloom, Kennedy did no work, answered no calls. He accepted the coward's lot: in escaping risk, you take the battering of the voices in your own mind.

And then he could take it no more. Eighty thousand North Vietnamese and NLF fighters attacked on the night of January 30, turning back American and South Vietnamese troops everywhere. For seven hours they even occupied the courtyard of the American embassy in the South Vietnamese capital of Saigon. Not only were the Americans failing to win the war, they were in danger of losing it.

The president could not face reality, overseas or in America, and the nation was suffering. Someone had to stop him. On March 10, Bobby hurried to join Cesar Chavez. For twenty-five days, Chavez had been on a hunger strike to force grape growers to bargain with his union. Kennedy came to stand by his side as he ended the fast. It was as if he needed to touch base with the most committed side of himself, with the person who best expressed his ideal of political courage, before he himself began his greatest fight.

On March 16, Bobby announced that he would run against the president for the Democratic Party nomination. That very same day, in Vietnam, American soldiers rampaged through the village of My Lai, killing over three hundred civilians. The public would not learn about My Lai for over a year, but when it did, the massacre came to stand for the very worst side of the war: Americans driven to senseless violence by fear and by prejudice. Violence had been a theme of Kennedy's whole political life: Freedom Riders beaten by the Klan; America's ghettos burning; the heart-stopping moments when the world stood at the brink of nuclear war; his brother assassinated; the ever-escalating deaths in Vietnam. On the most idealistic level, Bobby was running so that America would not be the land of the My Lai murders.

Kennedy's campaign was like the Atlantic City convention all over the country. He wasn't even just a rock star anymore; he was the symbol of hope, youth, and courage. If his brother had been Arthur, slain before his time, he was the young knight who could end the nightmare and bring back the dream. At Kansas State University, 15,000 white Midwestern kids screamed so loudly a veteran New York reporter thought it sounded like Niagara Falls. And the 17,000 frenzied students at the University of Kansas topped that. Kennedy was riding, or, more accurately, calling forth, a great wave of feeling, feeling against the war, against the dark mood of the country, against Johnson. And Johnson felt the tide of hatred coming at him.

Ever since the previous summer, Johnson had been thinking of withdrawing from the race. He had wanted his legacy to be the Great Society, but now it was the horrible Vietnam War. He later said that he was "tired of feeling rejected by the American people. I'm tired of waking up in the middle of the night worrying about the war." In March, just after Kennedy announced that he was running, the men Johnson trusted most told him the war could not be won.

On March 31, fifteen days after Kennedy announced that he was a candidate, Johnson announced that "I shall not seek, and I will not accept, the nomination of my party for another term as your President." The battle between Johnson and Kennedy was over. The great villain, the usurper who came to power on the hero's death, was gone. But where did that leave the young prince?

Kennedy was now running against McCarthy; against Vice President Humphrey, who took over for Johnson; and against the sure Republican candidate, Richard Nixon. That was his political challenge, but if he was the beacon of hope, he was also running against his times. On April 4, he was scheduled to speak in Indianapolis. At 6:00 P.M. that evening, Martin Luther King was shot in Memphis, and he died an hour later. The malignant cancer of violence was growing again.

On a gusty night where he was crisscrossed by the ominous shadows of nearby trees, Kennedy reported the terrible news to a gasping crowd in a black neighborhood. He was direct, personal: one man who had lost a brother talking to a people who had lost a leader. He urged the crowd not to turn to hatred, though he himself had that impulse. He told them how he had learned to deal with his grief, through the words of Aeschylus, which he quoted from memory. And then he charged them to return home, to pray, and to "dedicate ourselves to what the Greeks wrote so many years ago: to tame the savageness of man and to make gentle the life of this world." The question was whether, in 1968, America could tame its own savageness. That night Kennedy could not sleep, and talked openly about the chance that he would be killed.

Ever since Jack first ran for office, Kennedy campaigns had set a standard for a new kind of politics. Bobby's was no exception. He spent record amounts on public relations firms to get him the best posters, the best TV ads, the best campaign films. His advance men were brilliant at gathering crowds and whipping up their emotions, so that when Bobby arrived people went wild. But his campaign was also very different from the style of politics we have in the twenty-first century.

Bobby did not just try to please voters—he challenged them. Today both parties pay the closest attention to polls that track the preferences of many different types of voters. Then they hire marketing specialists to hold focus groups where they try out ideas and phrases to see what each key type of voter likes or dislikes. Democrat and Republican candidates alike are determined never to say anything that could disturb an important voting block, and if one does, they flood the airwaves, as well as the blogs and Web

Bobby speaking at the University of Mississippi Law School in March 1966. Four years earlier, he had forced the school to accept James Meredith as its first black student. Bobby looks clear and direct, yet somehow vulnerable, speaking to people who hated him.

sites, with so many explanations that the original flub is quickly blurred, confused, or drowned out. That was not how Bobby campaigned in 1968.

In April he came to Indiana University to give a speech at the medical school. Addressing an over-whelmingly white audience of future doctors, he preached the need to provide health care for the poor and the disadvantaged. Speaking to elite students who were working very hard, with the prospect of having a good living, he spoke about bringing food and jobs to the poor; he talked about the importance of clean air, about the need to discourage young people from smoking. Predictably, the students did not like what they heard, and the only enthusiastic response came from a black janitor, who yelled out, "We want Kennedy." When a student challenged Kennedy, asking who would pay for these grand plans, he simply said, "You." The crowd booed. And then he stopped talking about policy entirely, and confronted his audience. "I look around this room and I don't see many black faces who will become doctors. . . . It's the poor who carry the major burden in Vietnam. You sit here as white medical students, while black people carry the burden of the fighting in Vietnam." The hostile audience didn't like hearing that, but they admired Kennedy for being so direct, and by the end began to applaud.

Sounding liberal, even radical, was much more popular in 1968 than it is today, and Kennedy certainly knew that his antiwar supporters would like what he said. But he was also a man who believed in being direct and enjoyed confrontation. He would rather challenge a room full of doubters than try to please them.

Kennedy won in the Indiana primary, and again in

Nebraska, but McCarthy beat him in Oregon, at the time a very white, Protestant state. This was the first election a Kennedy had ever lost, and it meant Bobby absolutely had to win the next contest, in California. California was a melting pot, with many black, poor, and liberal voters likely to respond to his message. But shortly before the primary, Johnson pulled out his most damaging secret. He leaked files proving that it was Bobby who had requested that the FBI spy on Dr. King.

Bobby's team protected him in exactly the same way as he had covered up his brother's serious illness. An ally noticed that the accusation was sloppy about the difference between wiretapping (listening in on phones) and bugging (planting a listening device). Bobby had requested a wiretap; his press release correctly said he had never asked for bugging. But once again, the simple truth is Bobby lied.

Even if he had been more direct, the leak might not have hurt him. In the black community, there was a kind of sad, weary acceptance. People knew Hoover had pressured Kennedy. They knew the Kennedys were not entirely trustworthy, but Bobby was their best hope, and they had to forgive him.

The poet Nikki Giovanni worked for Bobby at the time, and met him once. She admired him for being "real." That did not mean he always told the truth. No politician does. Rather, she felt she was dealing with a real person—a man who could be tough, could be hard, could be practical, but who would tell you to your face what he could do and what he couldn't.

For those who admired Bobby and especially those who knew him personally, his best quality was exactly what Nikki noticed: he was a real, three-dimensional human being. Even his rough edges made him less plastic than almost any other politician. And yet he was, in his bones, a politician.

Kennedy and McCarthy were to hold a televised debate in California. In this tight race, there was a good chance that it would decide the outcome. Bobby poured every ounce of his restless energy into getting ready for the event. Night after night, he and his aides reviewed the likely questions and prepared the best answers. Bobby was running as hard as he could, as he had on the football fields, and as he did in helping elect his brother. Overconfident, McCarthy shared drinks with a friend and fellow poet.

Bobby's challenge was to indicate to blacks, Hispanics—all of the minority voters who turned out for his parades—that he understood them and was their only voice, while at the very same time signaling to white suburban voters that he was really one of them. He found a brilliant, devious way to do it. When McCarthy argued that poor blacks needed to find jobs in the suburbs, outside of their crumbling neighborhoods, Kennedy shot back, "You are going to take ten thousand black people and move them into Orange County." Orange County was, and is, wealthy, white, and conservative. Even as he was running as the white man who understood black rage, Bobby was telling white people that he would protect them from blacks, keep them far away.

Although McCarthy's team tried to protest after the debate, Bobby got it right once again. He scored points while people were watching, and his aides took care of the explanations after the fact.

Now that he was on the road and mingling with crowds, Kennedy was taking great risks. But he refused to take the danger seriously. "I'm not afraid of anybody. If things happen, they're going to happen." Bobby screamed these words at William Barry, a friend who was doing his best to protect him on the campaign trail. He actually insisted on cutting back the security around him, and was furious at Barry for taking precautions. This was no longer brave; it was willful, in fact reckless.

Running for president in 1968, Bobby and the crowd needed each other so much there seemed to be no barrier between them.

One way to see Bobby's recklessness is as a product of 1968: after Johnson's withdrawal, after the crowd frenzy, and, especially, after King's murder, Kennedy couldn't think anymore, he couldn't calculate. He just had to go where the wave would take him. He knew very well it might crash, but he was no longer in a state where he could be cautious. He was a prisoner of the tide.

But there is another way to make sense of Bobby's behavior on the campaign. Perhaps he hesitated so long about running because on some deep, basic level he did not feel he was a leader. He was not Joseph, nor Joe Jr., nor Jack. He tried, God how he tried, to be what others needed him to be. He met the crowds, he counted the delegate votes, he gave the speeches, he prepared for the debate. But maybe he knew, in his deepest sense of himself, that he was not up to the task. He whipped up the crowds, urged his followers to see him as their hope, their voice, their hero, while courting the death that would save him from having to lead them. He could organize a winning campaign, but he himself could not be a winner.

On the night of June 4, Kennedy won the California primary. At midnight he made a happy, though exhausted speech, then, true to form, set out to meet the workers and kitchen help in the Ambassador Hotel. There, Sirhan Sirhan, a mentally disturbed Palestinian angry at him for having worn a yarmulke, a Jewish prayer cap, at a campaign stop and for his support for Israel, shot a bullet directly into his brain. Robert Francis Kennedy died early in the morning of the following day.

Epilogue

WHO WAS BOBBY Kennedy, and what legacy did he leave behind? Joseph Kennedy asked to be judged by his family, and using that standard, he failed. He taught his sons to be fearless risk takers, which, at its worst, meant being reckless. His eldest son, groomed to be president, died trying to be a hero, perhaps pushed by competition with his nearest brother. Jack's presidency was undermined by the poisonous world of secrets he and Bobby spawned. When Bobby ran for president, he was such a fatalist that he was angry with a friend for trying to protect him. He dared death to find him, and it did.

After Bobby's death, Ted began to drink too much and, like Jack, he was involved with many women. On July 18, 1969, Mary Jo Kopechne, a secretary from Bobby's office, drowned in Ted's car. At a minimum he was drinking and planning to take her home. At worst, he may have left her in the water when she could still have been saved. The tawdry incident with its suggestion of sexual indulgence and cover-up captured the dark side of the Kennedy men, from Joseph on through his sons. Even in the next generation, one of Bobby's sons died of a drug overdose, and another in a skiing accident. Then Jack's son John Jr. died while piloting a plane in weather conditions he did not have the experience to navigate. Ted's son Patrick checked himself into a hospital to deal with his addictions. On a personal level, the price of the recklessness Joseph encouraged was shortened lives and moral weakness.

There is another way, though, to look at Joseph and his sons. Joseph's hard-driving determination and business skill made his family rich. The Kennedy clan then entered politics, where it took on, challenged, and defeated the old WASP elite. As they made space for themselves, the Kennedys then responded to other outsiders who were shut out of the mainstream of American life. The brave blacks and whites of the Civil Rights Movement forced the Kennedys to face up to the real distortions in the nation and try to right them. After his brother's death, Bobby continued this effort, seeking out the most ignored and unfortunate, and making their cause his.

At his best, Bobby, like his brother Jack, was a man of courage, dedicated to giving his all to make the world a better place. The children of wealth and privilege, the Kennedys did not have to worry about how to make a living, only how to make a difference. They embraced the opportunity.

Bobby Kennedy was not a saint. He was a flawed man. But what he and his brother accomplished was to give form to the idea that America can change, can be different, can pursue its ideals. In part that was an image, one they carefully created. But it was an image the nation needed, and which remains as an ideal for others to emulate. That aspect of Bobby's legacy is reflected in the awards given out by the Robert F. Kennedy Memorial, which honor writers, journalists, and human rights activists who tell the truth, even when it is difficult or dangerous. But to see his legacy in an award for courage and idealism is only half right.

Bobby lived in a time just before our own: a time of divisions between the Soviet Union and America, black and white, Dove and Hawk, young and old, public and private. We now live in the age of simultaneous media streams—and, looking back, it was this world that was really being born in Bobby's day. In 1962, the planet might have blown up if a Western Union bicycle messenger did not pedal fast enough to the Soviet embassy. Yet by 1968, the ARPANET was being built. The first e-mail was sent four years later. The Kennedys tried to ride the media and hide their problems. They did not realize that the media would have no boundaries.

Bobby Kennedy's short, eventful, and ultimately tragic life, you might say, was the transition from a time of secrets to one of exposure. We now know as much about his crippling flaws as his lofty aspirations. If he no longer looms as a pure Kennedy prince, that is all the better. For instead of an idol, he comes across as a dark, complex—and deeply human—human being.

Notes

BOOKS ABOUT THE Kennedys have come in four waves, and I found each useful. Books written by the Kennedys or published while they were alive are more like primary sources than histories—they are the stories the family and its friends wanted told. Shortly after first Jack's and then Robert's deaths, grieving aides, friends, and family members wrote memoirs meant to capture the magic of a vanished time and enshrine the martyred men. This second phase of books culminated in 1978 with Arthur Schlesinger Jr.'s *Robert Kennedy and His Times*. Schlesinger is an eminent historian who was also a close friend and adviser to the Kennedys. A marvelous resource for any researcher, his book nonetheless tells only part of the story.

In the 1980s and '90s the mainstream press took notice of rumors about the Kennedys that had previously been sidelined. This resulted in a tide of books whose approach is summarized by the title of one that came out in 1997: *The Dark Side of Camelot*. Seymour Hersh is a prizewinning investigative reporter, and the book is a perfect antidote to Schlesinger: it believes or at least treats seriously everything Schlesinger tended to disbelieve or dismiss.

By 2000, any historian writing about the Kennedys had to account for all sides of their characters. This resulted in books that were neither nostalgic nor accusatory, and wrestled with the complex history of the family. The best of these, published that year, is *Robert Kennedy: His Life*, by Evan Thomas. Thomas creates an insightful psychological portrait that has much to offer any student. I learned a great deal from it. Three years later the historian Robert Dallek published *An Unfinished Life: John F. Kennedy, 1917–1963*. While not as probing as Thomas's book, it tracks down all the rumors and then tries to make sense of the man. Those interested in the saga of the whole fascinating Kennedy clan can start with Doris Kearns Goodwin's 1987 *The Fitzgeralds and the Kennedys: An American Saga*. A fine video biography is *RFK*, directed by David Grubin.

INTRODUCTION

"Some men see . . .": Witcover, *85 Days*, 251.

CHAPTER ONE

"Runt" and "sissy": Thomas, *Robert Kennedy*, 30.

"It either showed . . .": Thompson and Myers, *Robert F. Kennedy*, 43.

"Nothing came easy . . .": Schlesinger, *Robert Kennedy*, 45.

"We were to . . . to be the best" and "We don't want . . .": Schlesinger, *Robert Kennedy*, 14.

"Daddy's look": Schlesinger, *Robert Kennedy*, 16.

"terrific, but we've . . .": Kennedy, *Times to Remember*, 104.

CHAPTER TWO

"lived serenely amid . . .": Kennedy, *Times*, 49.

"favorite" and "little pet": Thomas, *Robert Kennedy*, 30–31.

"The girls and boys . . .": Kennedy, *Times*, 104.

"ask how the state . . .": Kennedy, *Times*, 105.

"great spirit" and "unscrupulousness": Goodwin, *The Fitzgeralds and the Kennedys*, 471.

"I'll write you . . .": Schlesinger, *Robert Kennedy*, 26.

"I wish Dad . . .": Goodwin, *The Fitzgeralds and the Kennedys*, 638.

"You'll just have . . .": Schlesinger, *Robert Kennedy*, 31.

"Mrs. Kennedy's little . . .": Thomas, *Robert Kennedy*, 31.

"Democracy is finished . . .": Thomas, *Robert Kennedy*, 33.

"What I remember . . .": Newfield, *Robert Kennedy: A Memoir*, 33.

"He didn't look . . .": Thomas, *Robert Kennedy*, 31.

"a bird in a storm" and "Bobby certainly tried . . .": Schlesinger, *Robert Kennedy*, 43.

"played a whale . . .": Thomas, *Robert Kennedy*, 51.

CHAPTER THREE

"I wish to . . .": Schlesinger, *Robert Kennedy*, 58.

"Next to John . . .": Schlesinger, *Robert Kennedy*, 53.

"It was like . . .": Dallek, *An Unfinished Life*, 118.

"I can't see . . ." and "You take Bobby . . .": Thomas, *Robert Kennedy*, 49.

"If you were . . .": Schlesinger, *Robert Kennedy*, 67.

"We're going to . . .": Thomas, *Robert Kennedy*, 48.

CHAPTER FOUR

"don't get me . . .": Dallek, *An Unfinished Life*, 173.

"I'll just screw . . .": Thomas, *Robert Kennedy*, 59.

"pro-Communist": Oshinky, *A Conspiracy*, 32.

"I liked him . . .": Thompson and Myers, *Robert F. Kennedy*, 100.

CHAPTER FIVE

"He resembles me . . ." and "hates the same . . .": Whalen, *The Founding Father*, 457.

"to get him . . . fight right here?": Schlesinger, *Robert Kennedy*, 113. (I have trimmed the exchange but all of the quotations are accurate.)

"days of rage": Thomas, *Robert Kennedy*, 68.

"really, deeply, emotionally . . .": Thomas, *Robert Kennedy*, 75.

"The whole idea . . . had a cruel . . .": Thomas, *Robert Kennedy*, 181.

"Guys that tried . . .": Thomas, *Robert Kennedy*, 77.

"Hoffa was my . . .": Schlesinger, *Robert Kennedy*, 161.

"Would you tell . . . Mr. Giancana.": Schlesinger, *Robert Kennedy*, 165.

"You say that . . . for 36 years.": Schlesinger, *Robert Kennedy*, 179.

CHAPTER SIX

"Son, you've got . . .": Shesol, *Mutual Contempt*, 10.

"All right, Jack . . ." and "It's ridiculous that . . .": Schlesinger, *Robert Kennedy*, 193.

"How would you . . .": Thomas, *Robert Kennedy*, 90.

"disorganized": Dallek, *An Unfinished Life*, 249.

"the corner grocer . . .": Dallek, *An Unfinished Life*, 250.

"Come down here . . .": Schlesinger, *Robert Kennedy*, 195.

"I don't think . . .": Dallek, *An Unfinished Life*, 256.

"John F. Kennedy has . . . superb": *John Kennedy: Denying Addison Disease* (Web site)

"leaned over LBJ's . . .": Thomas, *Robert Kennedy*, 97.

"we can't miss . . .": Schlesinger, *Robert Kennedy*, 206.

CHAPTER SEVEN

"Ask not what . . .": http://www.americanrhetoric.com offers text and a recording of the speech.

"We were to . . .": Schlesinger, *Robert Kennedy*, 14.

"war on crime": Thomas, *Robert Kennedy*, 115.

CHAPTER EIGHT

"They shot the tires . . .": Raines, *My Soul Is Rested*, reproduced on *Riders for Freedom (1961)* Web site.

"Tell them to . . .": Schlesinger, *Robert Kennedy*, 295.

"We can't let . . .": *Immigrant Workers Freedom Ride Coalition* Web site.

"had better be . . .": Schlesinger, *Robert Kennedy*, 296.

"The passengers are . . .": Schlesinger, *Robert Kennedy*, 297.

"Stop beating that . . .": *James Zwerg Recalls His Freedom Ride* Web site.

"Mister, get away . . .": Schlesinger, *Robert Kennedy*, 297.

"My God . . . they're . . .": *Immigrant Workers Freedom Ride Coalition* Web site.

CHAPTER NINE

"We have some . . .": Thomas, *Robert Kennedy*, 209.

"Our major problem . . .": Dallek, *An Unfinished Life*, 547.

"go in hard": Thomas, *Robert Kennedy*, 213.

"We're going to . . .": Thomas, *Robert Kennedy*, 212.

"with intense but . . ." and "a real turning point . . .": Thomas, *Robert Kennedy*, 218.

"The 1930's taught . . .": Fursenko and Naftali, *"One Hell of a Gamble,"* 246

"How does it . . . doesn't it?": Dallek, *An Unfinished Life*, 560.

"R. Kennedy and his . . .": Fursenko and Naftali, *"One Hell of a Gamble,"* 249.

"hand went up . . . fellow just blinked . . .": Thomas, *Robert Kennedy*, 225.

"I'm older": *RFK: American Experience* Web site.

CHAPTER TEN

"religious crusade, a fight . . .": Chappell, "Religious Revivalism in the Civil Rights Movement."

"Bombingham": *Court TV: Crime Library* Web site.

"Oppressed people cannot . . ." and "injustice anywhere is . . .": King, "Letter from Birmingham Jail."

CHAPTER ELEVEN

"There's been so . . .": Thomas, *Robert Kennedy*, 276.

"I thought they'd . . .": Schlesinger, *Robert Kennedy*, 609.

"Why, God?": Thomas, *Robert Kennedy*, 278.

"The innocent suffer . . .": Thomas, *Robert Kennedy*, 285.
"And even in . . .": Thomas, *Robert Kennedy*, 287.

CHAPTER TWELVE

"When he shall . . .": Thomas, *Robert Kennedy*, 296.
"I'm a Beatle": Thomas, *Robert Kennedy*, 300.

CHAPTER THIRTEEN

"Burn, baby, burn": *Watts Riots: "Burn, baby, burn"* Web site.
"kids in trouble . . .": Thomas, *Robert Kennedy*, 306.
"I'd be a Communist . . .": Thomas, *Robert Kennedy*, 309.
"white radicals who . . ." and "a Catholic conservative": Steel, *In Love with Night*, 194.
"I suggest that . . .": Schlesinger, *Robert Kennedy*, 791.
"Human history numberless . . . oppression and resistance.": Schlesinger, *Robert Kennedy*, 746.
"destroy you and . . .": Shesol, *Mutual Contempt*, 366.
"Hawk, Dove—or Chicken . . .": Thomas, *Robert Kennedy*, 351.
"tired of feeling . . .": Shesol, *Mutual Contempt*, 437.
"I shall not . . .": Shesol, *Mutual Contempt*, 436.
"dedicate ourselves to . . .": Thomas, *Robert Kennedy*, 367.
"We want Kennedy . . . fighting in Vietnam": Schlesinger, *Robert Kennedy*, 882.
"real": personal communication from Ms. Giovanni.
"You are going . . .": Steel, *In Love with Night*, 185.
"I'm not afraid . . .": Schlesinger, *Robert Kennedy*, 901.

Bibliography

Chappell, David L. "Religious Revivalism in the Civil Rights Movement." *African American Review* 36 (Winter 2000). Reproduced in http://findarticles.com/p/articles/mi_m2838/15_4_36/ai_97515888/pg_4

Dallek, Robert. *An Unfinished Life: John F. Kennedy, 1917–1963.* Boston: Little, Brown, 2003.

Fursenko, Aleksandr, and Timothy Naftali. *"One Hell of a Gamble": Khrushchev, Castro, and Kennedy, 1958–1964.* New York: Norton, 1997.

Giovanni, Nikki. Personal communication, oral. No date.

Goodwin, Doris Kearns. *The Fitzgeralds and the Kennedys: An American Saga.* New York: St. Martins, 1987.

Grubin, David (director). *RFK.* Produced by David Grubin and Sarah Colt. WGBH Education Foundation and David Grubin Productions, 2004.

Kennedy, Rose Fitzgerald. *Times to Remember.* New York: Doubleday, 1974.

King, Martin Luther, Jr. "Letter from Birmingham Jail." In *Why We Can't Wait.* New York: Mentor Books, 1964. Reproduced on *The Martin Luther King, Jr., Research and Education Institute* Web site.

Newfield, Jack. *Robert Kennedy: A Memoir*. New York: Bantam, 1969.

Oshinsky, David M. *A Conspiracy So Immense: The World of Joe McCarthy*. New York: Free Press, 1983.

Raines, Howell. *My Soul Is Rested: Movement Days in the Deep South Remembered*. New York: Putnam, 1977. Reproduced on *Riders for Freedom (1961)* Web site.

Schlesinger, Arthur M. *Robert Kennedy and His Times*. New York: Ballantine, 1978.

Shesol, Jeff. *Mutual Contempt: Lyndon Johnson, Robert Kennedy, and the Feud that Defined a Decade*. New York: Norton, 1997.

Steel, Ronald. *In Love with Night: The American Romance with Robert Kennedy*. New York: Touchstone, 2000.

Thomas, Evan. *Robert Kennedy: His Life*. New York: Simon & Schuster, 2000.

Thompson, Robert E., and Hortense Myers. *Robert F. Kennedy: The Brother Within*. New York: Macmillan, 1962.

Whalen, Richard J. *The Founding Father: The Story of Jospeh P. Kennedy*. New York: New American Library, 1964.

Witcover, Jules. *85 Days: The Last Campaign of Robert Kennedy*. New York: Putnam, 1969. Reprint, New York: William Morrow, 1988.

WEB SITES

http://www.americanrhetoric.com
Excellent site for finding and listening to important political speeches.

Court TV: Crime Library:
http://www.crimelibrary.com/terrorists_spies/terrorists/
birmingham_church/index.html
How Birmingham got its nickname.

Immigrant Workers Freedom Ride Coalition:
http://www.iwfr.org/civilhistory.asp
Excellent site for civil rights history, with links to other sites.

James Zwerg Recalls His Freedom Ride:
www.beloit.edu/~libhome/Archives/papers/jzwerg.html
James Zwerg's own story.

John Kennedy: Denying Addison Disease:
http://www.doctorzebra.com/prez/z_x35addison_g.htm
Site with many links that report the Addison's disease story in
great detail.

The Martin Luther King, Jr., Research and Education Institute:
http://www.stanford.edu/group/King/
Excellent site for the works and speeches of Dr. King.

RFK: American Experience:
http://www.pbs.org/wgbh/amex/rfk/filmmore/pt.html
Transcript of a fine video biography of RFK.

Riders for Freedom (1961):
http://www-personal.umd.umich.edu/~ppennock/
docFreedomRide.htm
Oral histories related to the Freedom Rides.

Watts Riots: "Burn, Baby, Burn":
http://blogcritics.org/archives/2005/08/18/071347.php
The story of the phrase *Burn, baby, burn* and the Watts riots.

Index